Studying Arts and H

Studying Arts and Humanities

Catherine Bates
Abi Matthewman

Published by
PALGRAVE MACMILLAN
Houndmills, Basingstoke, Hampshire RG21 6XS and
175 Fifth Avenue, New York, N.Y. 10010
Companies and representatives throughout the world

PALGRAVE MACMILLAN is the global academic imprint of the
Palgrave Macmillan division of St. Martin's Press, LLC and of
Palgrave Macmillan Ltd. Macmillan® is a registered trademark
in the United States, United Kingdom and other countries.
Palgrave is a registered trademark in the European Union
and other countries.

ISBN-13: 978–0–230–20547–5

This book is printed on paper suitable for recycling and made from fully
managed and sustained forest sources. Logging, pulping and manufacturing
processes are expected to conform to the environmental regulations of the
country of origin.

A catalogue record for this book is available from the British Library.

A catalog record for this book is available from the Library of Congress.

10   9   8   7   6   5   4   3   2   1
18   17   16   15   14   13   12   11   10   09

Printed and bound in Great Britain by
CPI Antony Rowe, Chippenham and Eastbourne

UGL
1146402
hunt
2/23/10
Contents

Introduction

● What does this book do?

Studying at university gives you a valuable opportunity to develop skills which, as well as being a vital part of your degree, will also enhance your career prospects. Designed specifically for students in higher education focusing on Arts and Humanities subjects, *Studying Arts and Humanities* provides study skills support which will help you learn how to be a successful, engaged university student, able to acquire knowledge, think critically, research effectively and write convincingly. This book contains:

- ● Extensive advice on each of the main study skills areas.
- ● Examples of good practice to consider.
- ● Interactive exercises where you can test what you have learnt.
- ● Checklists and advice sheets of key areas which you can photocopy and build upon to create your own study skills portfolio.
- ● Many suggestions and guidelines about other useful resources you can turn to, including websites, databases, libraries and university support services.

● How does this book work?

We aim to provide advice for anyone undertaking Arts and Humanities studies at higher education level. We have grouped Arts and Humanities together because, although there is an element of each discipline which requires specific study skills, we want to think about the skills and strategies applicable *across* disciplines. Whether you are undertaking a single honours, a joint honours or an interdisciplinary degree, you will invariably engage with more than one subject. Most degrees require you to take an elective which is not in your primary area of study in the first year. It is also important to take into account that disciplines influence each other: no subject you study will be a sealed container. For example, studying English literature often involves considering historical and philosophical context; moreover, when thinking about Modernist poetry written in the 1920s it can be useful to compare it to Modern Art which was developing in a similar context – it can be fascinating to explore how these different artistic disciplines impacted upon each other. It is, therefore, useful to think about how Arts and Humanities subjects work together; this can help you bring your own coherence to a degree dealing with multiple and diverse ideas. We hope that through the advice it gives, and the examples and exercises it provides, *Studying Arts and Humanities* will help you approach your university studies with a confident enthusiasm. As well as providing advice on settling into a new degree and a new institution, we provide ideas which should help you get into a productive study routine, develop the variety of reading strategies you will need to approach the wide variety of texts you will come across, learn how to write effectively in an academic, critical style, and think about how to enhance your career prospects.

● What are the Arts and Humanities?

Arts subjects are all involved with thinking about different kinds of artistic, creative production within a historical, philosophical and aesthetic context. They can also include a practical element focused on the student's own production – it is beyond the remit of this book to address this aspect of the Arts. Arts subjects include:

English literature
Classics
Modern languages – which often involve the examination of the literature and art of the country studied
Music
Art and Design
The Performing Arts (including Theatre and Dance)

Humanities subjects consider the ways the world we live in has been discussed, represented, and influenced by humans. All humanities subjects require students to reflect upon how they themselves analyse and think about the world. They include:

English literature
History
Philosophy
Classics
Theology
Music
Art History

For explanation's sake we have distinguished between Arts and Humanities subjects. However, they overlap heavily as we hope the descriptions and list of subjects show. They both require you to be reflective, creative and analytical; you will develop your own approach to perceiving and thinking about numerous issues which affect the world we live in. This is what makes studying Arts and Humanities subjects so interesting and so useful for a large number of careers.

We hope you enjoy this book and find it a useful study companion!

● Acknowledgements

This book would not have been possible without the energy, creativity, advice and support of numerous friends, colleagues and students. We would like to thank, in particular, Simon Burrows, Tracy Hargreaves and Paul Cooke at the University of Leeds for utilising their extensive experience to support the formative stages of this project. Thanks is also due to Patrick Webster for his advice about teaching students to write clearly. Of the many students we have worked with over the years, we owe special thanks to those who allowed drafts of their work to be adapted and used as examples, these are: Kate Fahie, Tom Hixson, Michael Hughes and Patrick Wells. Many friends and colleagues have listened to and shared ideas; we are indebted especially to Susan Anderson, Kaley Kramer, David Stirrup, Gillian Roberts, Eric Langley, Marcel Swiboda, Dave Gunning and Emma Smith.

Finally, our thanks go to Gareth and Will; ever-supportive, ever providers of much-needed distraction.

CATHERINE BATES
ABI MATTHEWMAN

1 Adjusting to University Life

● Introduction

You've made it. You've passed your exams, and you've secured your place at university. Congratulations! The hard work has paid off and you can look forward to an exciting and challenging few years. As the summer draws to an end, you must start to consider the practicalities of adjusting to your new life. This chapter gives you the low-down on all the things that you need to organise, sort out, and think about before you arrive at uni. It also gives you some hints and tips on how to survive (and flourish!) during your first few weeks and months.

● On your way

What sort of student are you? Where have you come from and what has been your experience so far? Are you a 'traditional' student – 18 years old and just passed your A-Levels, first time away from home? Or are you one of the (increasing number of) non-traditional students: perhaps you are mature and want a change of career. Maybe you are retired and have a degree already, or have kids, or are from a different country, or have a full-time job and are studying in the city you've lived in all your life. The possible number of variations is, of course, endless. But the common thing that unites all first-year students is that you must all *make the transition* to university. You must all respond to the new challenges that face you, be they social, financial, academic or combinations of all these. Your life will shortly be changing quite dramatically whatever your prior experience.

In order to deal with this change, it is worth thinking about what will be challenging for *you* specifically, given your very particular background. Why have you chosen your university? It might be that you know that the university has an excellent reputation for the course that you are studying, or it might have nothing to do with the academic side at all. You might have chosen it because of its location: far from home/close to home/busy nightlife/close to countryside, or whatever. Before you arrive on Day One, have a think about the type of environment that you have been used to: are you moving from a small town or village to a big city? Is it a long way from home? Will you have to get yourself around by public transport, in a way that you haven't had to before? How are you going to look after yourself and stay safe? How long will it take to travel there, and how are you going to get home in the holidays?

Have a think about the everyday questions of survival, of making friends and of fending for yourself: can you cook your own (nutritious) food? Can you talk to people you don't know and make friends easily (remember, everyone finds this hard)? Can you keep track of your budget for a week? What about for a month or even a year?

Consider the academic side of things too: is it a completely new subject? Have you had a break from studying? Did you do better or worse in your exams than you expected? Perhaps you were the person who always came top of the class at school; how are you going to cope with being surrounded by those who are your equals, or your betters? Are you sick of being treated like a schoolchild and want to be taken seriously? Are you excited and ready to engage in academic work in a completely new way?

Given all the new things that you are likely to experience, you may be feeling a sense of anticipation and excitement. Equally, you may be feeling anxious about the unknown. Everyone, to some degree, has *something* that they are worried about before starting university; facing up to those worries is a good start in overcoming them. What are *you* anxious about, in particular? More likely than not you will find someone in your first few weeks who feels exactly the same as you.

- Worried about living in a flat with strangers?
- Think you won't be able to find your way around campus or the town/city?
- Not sure that you have the same academic ability as the other students on your course?

These types of concerns are absolutely natural, but if you feel these worries are getting out of proportion, you need to remind yourself of all the great reasons why you are going to university – the freedom; the opportunity to broaden your horizons; the chance to meet many different types of people; to make new (sometimes lifelong) friends; to have fun; to learn; to challenge your intellect; to gain new skills and to prepare for your future!

Still, if these anxious thoughts linger, read on and you will see that there are a number of ways in which you can prepare yourself for university, and many opportunities to receive support, guidance or advice.

● Orientation

You will no doubt receive lots of information from your university before you arrive – sometimes this might seem like information overload, so you need to be selective about which bits you choose to read first. What are the things that you think are most important to know before you start?

> **Accommodation Checklist**
> - Do you know where you will be living?
> - Is it close to campus?
> - Do you know if it is on a bus route?
> - What is supplied in your accommodation package?
> - Have you been given a map?
> - When and where can you collect your key?

The first thing that you will need to do is sort out your accommodation. This might be relatively straightforward, for example, if you are staying in university halls of residence. However you will still need to find your hall (Is it on- or off-campus? Can you drive up to the front door?) and get your key (Have you got the paperwork that the accommodation office sent you?). If you haven't lined up your accommodation before you arrive, then there will probably be a period of temporary accommodation until you find something more permanent. The university will be able to point you in the direction of private landlords who rent to students; many will have websites with vacancies listed.

Getting yourself moved into your student house or halls is a priority; you will find that the local supermarket and shops are *full* of new students, buying washing up liquid, bin bags, batteries, tea, coffee and all those things that you forgot to pack. This is a great opportunity to get to know your fellow flatmates. You could suggest that you go to the shops *en masse* and buy all your communal items. You never know, deciding what toilet roll to buy might end up being a truly bonding experience. (If you're unlucky, it might also highlight any potential issues with personality clashes. My advice would be to try not to have an argument on your first outing as a house to the shops.)

● Around campus

After you have sorted out your living arrangements, you'll need to ensure you know where the university is and how to get to it. You should be able to find details of bus routes and cycle paths online and, if you intend to walk, a quick look at a map might be in order if the route is not obvious. If you are bringing a car to university, make sure you check whether students can park on campus, and how much this costs. You may have already visited the university before you applied: now is the time to reacquaint yourself with the campus. For example, you'll probably need to locate your department, the Students' Union, the bookshop, the lecture theatres, the library and the sports centre. There are likely to be organised tours of the campus going on in the first week or so. Sign yourself up to one if you are feeling a little disoriented. A campus tour is also a good way to meet people beyond your halls of residence.

● Making friends

It would be fair to say that the most daunting thing about starting university is likely to be moving beyond familiar surroundings and facing the prospect of having to make new friends. Many people worry about whether they'll get on with their new flat-mates or course-mates and wonder whether the friends that they make at uni will be as close as the ones they already have. Remember that the friends you have back home are ones that you have made over a period of months or even years. You *will* make friends at uni – and lasting friendships at that – it might just take a bit of time. People you meet on your first day or in the first week might not be the people you end up spending time with. You should expect a few awkward 'introductory' conversations (in my experience these all take the same form – so brace yourself for a bit of repetition): 'Where are you from? What A Levels did you do? Where are you living?' etc. Everyone is going through the same experience, but people cope with these situations in different ways. Some might be very socially outgoing and happy talking to new people; some might appear confident and want to show off, but perhaps hide a lack of confidence or anxiety about meeting new people; some might not want to be the first to make conversation and prefer to keep quiet for a bit.

However you cope with these situations, a bit of time and openness will see you through. A good way to pre-empt awkward first encounters before you start uni is by joining social networks before you arrive: your department's Society is bound to have something happening online; your course itself might have some way of contacting course-mates; if your hall hasn't got an online group before you arrive, why don't you set one up? You can swap information and advice and arrange to meet up with people before you even arrive.

A lot of people feel that they lack confidence when meeting a new group of people, and it is common to feel that everyone else has made friends already and that you've somehow been left behind. If you feel like this in your first week or so, remind yourself that *everyone* is new and that *no-one* can make lifelong friends in a matter of a week! If you have friends who are also new to uni, give them a ring to see how they are finding life in the first few weeks. There will be time for you to find a new friendship circle, but it can be hard at first: sometimes you'll have to grit your teeth and get through the awkward bits. Once you have found some people with whom you have things in common, the embarrassing social encounters will get fewer and fewer.

> If you are feeling lonely and don't think you can get over your feeling of loneliness, find your personal tutor or go the university's student counsellor. There will be someone on site whose job it is to see if you are OK, and to whom you can talk in confidence.

● Freshers' Week

Your university will probably have a 'Freshers' Week' for new students, before lectures begin for real. During this week you will meet staff in your department along with the other students on your programme, and do all the boring but necessary paperwork – sign up and register for your academic course modules; get your student union card sorted; maybe have a tour around the campus and work out where the important buildings are, and so on. In addition to the daytime activities that will be laid on, there will probably be lots of social events in the evenings. The Students' Union will be advertising itself as the place to meet friends, join societies, sign up for voluntary work and drink in the bar. Pubs and clubs in the town/city will probably be having low-priced drinks promotions in time for the new term in an attempt to lure you into their establishments. There may be a 'Societies' Fair' where university societies set out their stalls to attract new members. You will almost certainly find a society that interests you – all tastes, faiths, sports and interests are catered for – even if it is just your own departmental society. Now is a good time to sign up and join – when lots of other people are new to it too. Societies are a great way to meet people that you have something in common with, besides your course or your halls of residence.

● Socialising

It is a bit of a tradition that Freshers' Week tends to be a riotous affair, with much socialising, going out, and partying. After all, the real work hasn't started yet, so there are no 9 o'clock lectures to get up for. Enjoy yourself during Freshers' Week and take the opportunity to meet new people and have fun. If you drink alcohol and intend to socialise at pubs and bars, take some commonsense precautions: know how to get home safely, have a phone number for a licensed taxicab company handy, and most importantly, know your limits. Ending up in police cell or in A&E is not fun, whichever way you look at it.

Be considerate of your fellow housemates who may choose to abstain from drinking for cultural, religious or other reasons. It is pretty horrible being woken up by drunken revellers in the early hours and will not make for a happy household.

● Homesickness

Your first few weeks are likely to be a heady mixture of emotional highs and lows as you begin your new course. The excitement of making new friends, experiencing a new institution, and perhaps a new town or city and beginning your degree may bring with it some accompanied feelings of disappointment, anxiety and worry about the new challenges that you face. Plus you are likely to be missing your family and friends, if they are 'back home'. This is completely understandable, even for students who couldn't wait to get away. Make sure you keep in touch with your friends and family. Plan and pay for your visits home early: by booking your tickets in advance you'll have something to look forward to and avoid the risk of running out of money by the end of term! The holidays will come round very quickly, and you never know, during your Christmas break you might start missing your friends from uni and long for the freedom and independence that you enjoyed whilst studying with others.

● Finances, fees and loans

Things seem to be ever-changing in the world of student finances; what we know at the moment (2009/10) is that the tuition fees are certainly not getting any cheaper. Before you arrive at university, you and anyone else involved with paying your fees will have to negotiate your way around the rather daunting world of student loans, maintenance grants and bursaries. The good news is that that there is money available for the people who need it most; not all of it must be paid back, but a good chunk of it will be repaid to the Student Loans Company once you graduate and earn over £15K per year. There are resources online that will help: see www.direct.gov.uk/ for more information. Once your family's income has been assessed, you will be told how much your tuition fees are, what your loan entitlement is, and whether you qualify for a bursary. Find out exactly when your tuition fees must be paid, and what payment options your university provides: a delay in paying the fee may result in late registration for your course; on the other hand, you may get the chance to pay in instalments, or find out it is cheaper to pay it all at the beginning.

Opening a Bank Account

Do some basic research into what the banks are offering to students: most will offer free overdrafts, debit cards, and most likely credit cards and freebies too, to win your custom. Try to find a bank that is close to campus, so if you have any problems you can speak to someone in person. You'll be able to open a bank account with some ID, your offer letter from the university and a letter showing your address.

Remember: even if banks are offering credit cards with low interest rates, these rates are likely to be low for only a limited period. As soon as you start spending on a credit card, you have to start repaying: if you think you can survive without a credit card, then refuse the bank's offer. You are not obliged to take everything they throw at you!

● Managing on a budget

Whatever your financial status, it is unlikely that you will have limitless amounts of cash, so you will need to give some thought to your budget. Some of this may have been decided for you already; if you have chosen to live in halls or fixed rent accommodation you will be able to calculate your rent for the year, and if you are in catered halls, then part of your food budget will already have been eaten up. Your university will be able to provide some indication of the living costs in your area of the country. London is notoriously expensive, whereas university towns in the north of the country may provide better value for money. You may want to work part-time to supplement your income. If so, remind yourself that a commitment to a part-time job during your studies, even if you are working in a shop or a bar, will stand you in good stead when you apply for graduate jobs later on. Try not to over-commit yourself to working a lot of hours right at the start of term. If you can, give yourself time to get used to your new uni routine, and make sure you know when periods of assessments and deadlines for essays are, so that you can plan your part-time work around these.

So, you should by now have a rough idea of the amount of money that you've got for the year. What you must do now is break this down into manageable chunks, and try to come up with a rough weekly amount that you can live on. Find out when you need to pay your major expenses such as your fees, rent and bond/deposit. Check when you receive the instalments of your loan, grant or bursary, and make sure you mark this in a diary/wall planner or calendar: something that you look at *often*, so that you can get a feel for the number of weeks that you must survive on the cash that you have in your account.

Overdraft Alert!
Ensure that you are registered for your bank's online service, so that you can check your whole statement at any time; get into the habit of checking your online statement at least once a week to see where all your money goes! Believe me, the worst feeling is when you've run out of bread and milk and the cash machine won't even let you have £10. Being reduced to collecting the coppers that have fallen out of your wallet and that have collected at the bottom of your bag is a demoralising experience, so make sure you know exactly what's happening in your account. If you have an overdraft facility on your student account, you will be charged interest (at the very least) on the amount by which you exceed the overdraft and may well be given a fine. This can be particularly soul-destroying when you haven't checked your balance and don't realise that you keep going over your limit, and keep getting charged the bank's fines.

Once you know your big expenses, you'll have to think about the items that you need to be able to start your course; **reading lists** will contain all the books that you are expected to either borrow from the library or purchase (and read!). Get to the library as early in your course as possible, because there will only be a limited number of course texts available. You might find that these are restricted to a shorter loan period too. Bear in mind that many courses cover the same texts from year to year, so make sure you check the notice boards around your department for second years selling their old books at knock-down prices. Go to second-hand bookshops, or search for second-hand books on websites such as Amazon and Abebooks but make sure you buy the edition or translation of the book that is specified on the reading list. You don't want to end up having to buy the book twice because you got it wrong the first time. Some of the time you *will* have to buy a new copy of the text in question, but if you try to limit this as much as possible, you will save pounds.

If you have moved to a new place to study, at the start of term you will also need to buy all those essential items for your house or flat. Financial matters are notoriously difficult to negotiate with friends or housemates, so tread carefully. You may want to set up a **house kitty** for communal items, but *do* expect at least one person *never* to contribute to it! This sort of thing can cause real ill-feeling within a house, so make sure you cough up your share, and take your turn to shop for washing-up liquid or bin-bags or whatever it may be. You'll probably buy your own food, but you may want to share everyday items like milk and sugar. A good idea might be to invest in a marker pen so that you can write your name in big letters on your favourite yoghurt. At least that way, people are less inclined to steal it, when it is obvious that it does not belong to them. All of this might sound a bit petty, but if new to it, you need to prepare yourself for the delights of communal living. It might be an idea to have a think about how you would respond to situations like these before they (inevitably) happen. I have heard of house wars over food and – perhaps less surprisingly – over alcohol going missing in mysterious circumstances.

Week to week you will need to weigh up how much cash you have for socialising, food, clothes, travel and hobbies. You might have to make cutbacks in some areas, but do not sacrifice your own personal safety in order to save money. For example, if you are out on the town after dark (especially if you are a woman), never walk home on your own – and when you are walking around don't make obvious desirable belongings people may want to steal such as expensive mobile phones and MP3 players: make sure you reserve enough money for your taxi or late bus ticket. There are some good ways of saving money: when it comes to food, consider buying your fresh fruit and veg from the market instead of more expensive convenience stores, and learn to cook some new recipes instead of buying ready-meals. There are many good books out there designed to help you cook healthily on a budget. Plan your meals in advance so that you can use up ingredients in more than one meal, and get some freezer bags so that you can keep left-overs. Take advantage of the cheap deals on offer in your local supermarket or students' union. As for travel, investigate money-saving student travel cards, weekly or monthly bus tickets, and always try to book train travel early when you'll be able to get the cheapest deals. If you are shopping for clothes, CDs or DVDs, look out for the many shops that offer 10% discount to students.

> **Top Tip for Surviving on a Budget**
> Once you have worked out your basic weekly budget (for food, travel and socialising) withdraw this amount **in cash** from your bank on the **same day each week**. By using cash you will be able to keep track of how much you are spending. This is *much* harder to monitor when you use debit or credit cards – especially if there is alcohol involved!

● Sorting out the paperwork

In your first week or so, you will be responsible for getting registered for your course and sorting out the necessary paperwork that means that you can begin studying your chosen subject. Many universities operate on a 'modular' system whereby the course is split into smaller chunks which are each worth a certain amount of credit. For example, one module that lasts for one semester or term might be worth 10 credits. Over the whole year you might need to pass 120 credits. This will vary from one institution to another, and will of course depend on what you are studying, and whether it is an honours degree, a normal degree, a diploma or certificate. Find out what system operates at your institution: universities tend to be huge bureaucratic beasts, and you will find that there is a process that you must go through in order to make sure your paperwork is in order. Fortunately, most universities are moving towards online registration, meaning that you can manage your own account and view your options at a computer, rather than having to queue at an office. Watch out for notices about modules fairs that you can attend in person, however. These fairs are especially useful if you have the option of choosing 'elective' modules – ones outside your core curriculum, or even department. Modules fairs give you the opportunity to meet with academics and departments and get a feel for what's on offer from around the university – even in subjects that you previously hadn't considered studying.

Other things to sort out in the first week or so include getting your Student Card and Library Card (they may be the same thing); finding out how to sign up for tutorials and seminars; and researching the location of your first lectures.

● What will study be like? The 6 hours trap

So, what do you expect university work to be like? It is certainly very different from school, but in what way? In the Arts and Humanities in particular, more so than any other discipline, you will find that you are expected to study *independently*. You'll come across this word a lot. What does it mean in practice? Well, it means that there will be some scheduled classes during the week, but you will find, perhaps with some shock (and delight?), that your timetable looks very, very *empty* when you first arrive. What's your reaction to the thought that you might only have **six hours** per week of scheduled contact time with your lecturers and tutors? Perhaps your initial thought is 'Great!' – more time for sport, sitting in the pub or recovering from the night before, earning money, watching *Neighbours*, or whatever your preferred leisure-time pursuit may be. If this is what you are secretly thinking, then it is probably fair to say that many, many people think the same thing. From my experience, this seems to be the default position of *most* new students.

The *problem* is that some students never get out of this mode of thinking: they think that university is the thing that you 'turn up' for, like you used to turn up to school. These students, unless preternaturally gifted, are the types of students who leave university with poor degrees. It's really sad to see intelligent students like these *entirely missing the point* of studying at university, and studying in the Arts in particular. Yes, of course you can coast through if you want; you might be lucky and not come completely unstuck by the end of your degree, but you will almost certainly have a *greatly impoverished* experience of academic life.

Of course, I think this will only apply to a minority. After all, you have chosen to study a degree in the Arts and Humanities because you love the subject, right? And you want to pursue it in greater depth; you are excited at the prospect of exploring your subject further and getting the chance, perhaps, to specialise in an area that you find exciting, intriguing, challenging and inspiring. Nevertheless, even if you are intellectually 'turned on' by your subject, I should warn you that it is very easy to forget that what is expected of you at university will be very different. That is, it is incredibly easy to fall into the 6 hours trap – only 'working' when you turn up at your lectures and seminars with the addition of cramming for exams and writing your essays at the last minute. And why is that? Why is it easy, even for motivated and conscientious students, to find themselves working in this way? *Because no one will remind you that you should be working every day – not even your lecturers!*

No one is going to nag you to go to the library and read, or sit at your desk and plan your working week. Lecturers and tutors will not be checking up on you every week or even asking to see any evidence of work. At the beginning of your course you *will* be provided with some information of what is expected of you – the times and venues of your lectures, perhaps the dates of when your assignments are due, or when your exams will be, but it is no one else's responsibility to make sure that you have taken any of this information in. So, for example, you've read your lecture timetable, but have you got to go and sign up to a seminar group yourself? Must you go in person to the department's office, or can you do it online? I have had students who didn't turn up to seminars until Week 5 of the course because it took them that long to realise that it was something that they should have sorted for themselves.

So there's the warning. Later in this book I offer some thoughts on how to avoid becoming one of those students who fall into the 6 hours trap. And I hope you will see that I am not advocating that you give up your social life or the opportunities to get involved with all the extra-curricular delights that are available on- and off-campus; I'm suggesting that there is a balance to strike, and a bit of planning and organisation to think about. You will enjoy your leisure time even more knowing that your academic life is on track. You will be able to have fun without feeling guilty that you aren't in the library (what a terrible thought!) and, most importantly, you will be able to make the most of your time at university and come out with a decent degree at the end of it.

● Organising a timetable

Your academic year is likely to be divided up into terms or semesters and these will determine when your periods of teaching, exams, assessments and holidays will fall. For example, your university year might begin in October with 11 weeks of teaching in the period before the Christmas break, followed by a period of exams afterwards, and so on. Try to get an idea of how your university's calendar works, noting down any important dates and deadlines and closure days.

When it comes to getting organised, different methods suit different people, but you need some way of planning your time, particularly so if you have a part-time job too. It could be a simple academic diary, calendar, wall chart, Blackberry or Outlook Calendar: something that suits your lifestyle, which you can refer to quickly and easily. Don't expect to be able to hold all the times of your lectures, seminars, deadlines, holidays, exams in your head at once. By putting them down on paper, or on screen, you will be able to see at a glance what you need to prepare for, and what you have coming up. Hopefully, that way you will avoid any nasty shocks. Work carefully through the documentation relating to each of your modules (most useful will be the 'Module Handbook' or its equivalent). You will find that this contains a lot of information that you need to transfer into your diary, including essay deadlines and exam periods. Once you have done this, you will be able to see the times when you'll be busiest during your week, and during the semester.

On a week-to-week basis you'll need to give some thought to when and where you work best, beyond your lectures and seminars. Some people are at their most alert and effective in the mornings, whereas others are better in the evenings. Remember your working week will include all sorts of different tasks: some will be *extremely cerebral*, and will require some deep and careful thought on your part. Other tasks will be less demanding. Try to schedule your most difficult tasks for when you know you work at your best. Your environment, too, will affect the quality and quantity of your work. Where do you find it easy to concentrate? What distractions do you need to avoid? Have a think about the type of task you are doing; do you really need to be somewhere with an internet connection when you are reading, or is this likely to prove distracting? How noisy is it in your bedroom? Will your friends/family leave you in peace, or will they be bugging you to join in with their activities? What are your university's library facilities like? Can you work comfortably in there? When you know the tasks, activities or assignments that you should be doing, make a note in your diary about *where* and *when* you plan to get them done. Figure 1.1 shows an example of such a schedule.

When you look at the whole term, semester or year, you'll be able to see when your major pieces of assessed work are due. Mark in these deadlines, and consider how close together they are; one of the hardest things you'll find is that essays for different modules may all come around the same time. If you are the type of person who tends to leave everything to the last

Day/Time	Monday	Tuesday	Wednesday	Thursday	Friday
9:00	# Intro to 20th Cent. Poetry LECTURE Room 121, English Dept.				
10:00			# Intro to Moral Philosophy, LECTURE, Lecture Theatre 31, Adam Smith Building.		# Philosophy of Literature TUTORIAL, Seminar Room 23, School of Philosophy
11:00		* Dr Hargreaves' Personal Tutor Office Hour, Room 233, English Dept.		£ Work @ SuperFoods	
12:00		* Essay Writing Workshop (Remember to Sign UP!) Skills Centre	# The 19th Century Novel, LECTURE, Lecture Theatre 22, Adam Smith Building	£ Work @ SuperFoods	# The 19th Century Novel, SEMINAR, (odd weeks) Room 2, English Dept.
13:00	# Philosophy of Literature, LECTURE, Lecture Theatre A, Chemistry Dept.	@SWIM SOC!	# Intro to 20th Cent. Poetry SEMINAR (even weeks) Dr Bates' office (Room 227)	£ Work @ SuperFoods	
14:00		@SWIM SOC!		£ Work @ SuperFoods	
15:00	* Library Skills Training (Drop-In)			£ Work @ SuperFoods	
16:00	* Library Skills Training (Drop-In)			£ Work @ SuperFoods	
17:00				£ Work @ SuperFoods	

\# Lectures, seminars and tutorials
* Things that are useful for your academic life, but not compulsory

£ Paid part-time work
© Scheduled co-curricular activities

Unshaded areas Free time? Or 25 hours' worth of reading, researching, writing up lecture notes, drafting essays and preparing for assignment

Figure 1.1

minute (and many people are), watch out for these clashing deadlines. You may have to re-think your strategy and plan the weeks and days beforehand very carefully.

● Planning for time off and relaxation

Once you've got your semester's work planned out as much as possible, you'll be able to see when and where your workload should be relatively 'light' i.e. not around deadlines. In order to reward yourself and to have something to look forward to, you may want to plan some time off for visiting friends or going home. Find out whether your course has a 'Reading Week' in the middle of the semester when you don't have any lectures or seminars; don't presume that you do, just because your friends on a different course have one, as it might vary from department to department.

● Personal tutoring

Many universities operate a 'personal tutoring' system where you are assigned to a member of staff in your department. The system varies from one university to another, but more often than not this is a person who may not necessarily teach on any of your modules, but to whom you can go to discuss any aspect of your academic work. Your personal tutor should communicate the times that they are available to be seen; go and find their office and see whether they have posted a notice on their door. Introducing yourself to your personal tutor is your responsibility: don't expect them to come looking for you! Try to get as much as possible out of your meetings with your personal tutor; you should prepare what you want to talk about before you see them, and jot down any questions you want to ask so that you don't forget. Some students find meetings with personal tutors intimidating due to their one-to-one nature, but try to remember that tutors are there to help you. They know that you are not (yet!) an expert in your discipline, and that you are in the early stages of your academic career. They will not put you on the spot or test you, but they might ask you some probing questions to get you thinking. There is no shame in saying 'I don't know, but I'll have a think about it.' After all, thinking is going to play a major part in your academic education.

Some personal tutors also provide pastoral support; you can go to them if you are experiencing difficulties that are unrelated to your academic work, such as when you are unwell or you have some personal issues that you want to discuss in confidence. It is worth finding out what system operates in your department; it might be the case that pastoral support can be found elsewhere, perhaps from a dedicated student support officer.

● Changing modules and programmes

If you are not enjoying your course in the first few weeks, your personal tutor is probably the best person to talk to as they will be able to give you a bit more perspective about your degree as a whole. If there is something specific that you are struggling with, then they will know whether this is something that forms a core part of your degree programme or whether this is merely a feature of the early stages of the course. Your personal tutor can also give you an indication of the modules that are available to you in your second and third year, where opportunities to specialise in a certain area may be greater.

● Student support services

If you are struggling, for any reason, in your first few weeks and months at university, there *will* be dedicated services on campus that you can access for support. Some students feel as though they are somehow undeserving of this support, that it's 'not for them'. Be sure to know that the university or students' union will have an equal access policy for all their support services: if you are in need, then there will be someone who can help, give advice and guidance whether this is for academic, social, financial, housing,

---

Examples of student support services
Medical Practice
Counselling Service
Library Staff and Training
Study Skills Help/ Writing Centre
Housing/Accommodation Office
Students' Union (for advocacy, academic appeals etc.)
Careers Service
International Students' Office
Lifelong Learning/Continuing Education Office

or personal support. You might have to do some research in tracking down where these support services can be found, but all are likely to have links from the university's website, or contact numbers in your student handbook. There is no reason for you to worry or suffer alone: find out who you can speak to and where they are based, and get some help.

● Summary

This chapter has given you taste of what studying at university will be like. **Making the transition** to university will be different for everyone, no matter what your background. There are many challenges to be faced: a new environment; perhaps living away from home; sorting out your finances; **surviving on a budget** and settling in to a new way of doing things. These challenges also present new opportunities: to start afresh; **to get organised**; to make new friends and to get excited about **studying in a new way** and in a new context. The rest of this book will help you think about the way in which you study, and study the Arts and Humanities in particular. These disciplines are difficult, but they are also extremely rewarding: you must rely on your own enthusiasm, determination and intellect in order to get the most out of them. Don't expect your lecturers to tell you how, or where, or when, to think! They won't give you model answers for passing exams (and you won't get that from this book either, I'm afraid), but that doesn't mean that your lecturers and tutors won't support you in your academic development – far from it. You will be given feedback on your work and on your ideas, and encouragement to pursue new lines of thought and enquiry. Don't forget that there are many **support services** that can help you if you are experiencing a specific difficulty. In the end, though, the buck stops with you: your degree is what *you* make of it. Students who do well in the Arts and Humanities, who come out with a top degree, are the ones who have taken responsibility for their own academic development and are independent, motivated, enquiring and ready to learn.

2 Becoming a University Student

● Introduction

As Chapter 1 stressed, one of the difficult but exciting aspects of adjusting to university life is the expectation from your tutors that you will do most of your learning independently. Rather than relying on your tutors to provide the majority of the resources, you will be asked to develop your own ideas in lectures, seminars, oral presentations and written assignments. You will also be expected to find materials to supplement your learning and guide your thinking; the two key places you will find these are your university library and the internet. These can both be quite overwhelming places in which to search for information, so you will need to develop strategies to find the information you require, as well as making sure the sources you consult are relevant, useful, and reliable.

This chapter will deal first with some suggestions about how to get into an effective study routine, thinking about how you can start as you mean to go on: as a productive student who gets work done in a calm and relaxed manner! It will then go through some ways to approach familiarising yourself with what a rich resource your university library is, both in the physical books, journals, newspapers and other media it holds as well as the electronic resources it makes available to you. Next, it will suggest some ways for you to assess whether the information is reliable enough to be used as a source for an academic essay; the internet is an infinitely useful resource but since it is unselective and unedited, it needs to be treated with care. Finally, this chapter will help you think about how to get the most out of the contact time an Arts degree *does* provide: it will help you think about how to approach lectures, seminars and personal tutorials, and to consider how to prepare for them effectively, interact in them and, most importantly, how to follow up the useful learning they provide.

● Developing effective study habits

Coming to university, living with different people, taking lots of different modules, and working with a variety of tutors, can all be a bit unsettling at the beginning. For some it is very exciting, and it is easy to lose focus on the work with all the opportunities for socialising. For others, it becomes overwhelming, with deadlines piling up rapidly: the emphasis put on independent learning can seem unsupportive, but there are many places you can find support – the onus is on you to find them (Chapter 1 can help you with this). However, with or without the search for extra help it is helpful to try and gain control yourself by developing some kind of routine. A routine will ensure that the work and preparation you need to do is undertaken in a relatively calm manner. If you can avoid letting things pile up, by leaving everything to the last minute, you will give yourself more of a chance to understand, develop and so enjoy your subjects.

Here are some rules of thumb which should help you come up with some useful study habits.

Work regularly and don't let the deadlines pile up

If you think of your degree as a job, then you will realise that each day you should be working about 7 or 8 hours a day, 5 days a week (in which you can get much done, but which should allow for big breaks and weekends off, if you make these hours work for you). This amount of work will enable you to keep up with seminar preparation and reading for lectures and so will help you feel more confident about the first assignments. In other words, it is a good idea to study throughout the semester, rather than only looking at the reading list for specific assignments.

Find some good study spaces

You are much more likely to get down to studying quickly, and happily, if you find places you feel comfortable working in. This could be at home in your room or it could be in the library. It may be that you need a few different places to study – some people get restless in one place, others prefer to set up their study space and always work there. It is a good idea not to get too attached to a place, though, because there will be times when you may need to study elsewhere – your usual spot may get disrupted. So, I always have a few back-up plans. Just make sure you find a place where you:

- Have enough light.
- Have enough space.
- Won't get disrupted continually (e.g. you might want to find a hiding place in the library, or – if you like background noise – a café which your best friends don't necessarily know about).

● Have access to regularly – don't set your heart on working on the same computers in the university library if you always have to queue for them; this is frustrating and wastes time. Try and get there early enough to avoid the queues, or, when in university, find work to do which does not involve the computer.

It is important to find a place in which you can concentrate – hours can be wasted trying to work somewhere with constant disruption. If you are a procrastinator, it is even more vital that you try to find somewhere free from distractions.

Get into the habit of working out what needs doing when

Prioritising your work tasks can take a lot of organisation and time, but is really worth doing – otherwise you could find yourself putting much work into one area of study, and realising the deadline for another assignment is looming and you have not thought about it. This is actually a study skill which will become a necessary work skill in whatever career you choose to undertake. It can be useful to do weekly timetables to help you make sure you know what is getting done when. First, write down all the preparation which needs doing, dividing into subject and estimating the time it will take to do each task. Then you can start seeing where this could fit into both a weekly and a monthly timetable.

Look at the example of Katie who is taking Philosophy and Art History. She has the following commitments:

Philosophy   *The Mind* – 2 lectures and 1 seminar a week. Assessment: 2 essays and 1 exam (at end of the module)
Enlightenment Epistemologies – 2 lectures and 1 seminar a week. Assessment: 2 essays and 1 exam (at end of the module)

Art History   *Renaissance Art* – 2 lectures a week; 1 2-hour seminar every other week. Assessment: Weekly assessed 200 word critiques, 1 essay and 1 exam.

Katie has drawn up the weekly timetable shown in Figure 2.1.

This timetable fits in much time for work, but also a substantial amount of time for socialising and extra-curricular activities. It is also designed to be flexible – the time chunks can be swapped around if something unexpected occurs. For example, if a friend visits on a Friday, Wednesday afternoon and evening could be spent working. Katie is trying to make the most of her time by planning to work between lectures and seminars – in this way she

	Monday	Tuesday	Wednesday	Thursday	Friday	Saturday	Sunday
Morning 9–1	Reading for RA seminar and lecture – in library to help concentration	9–11 Mind/ EE reading: library 11–12 Mind lecture	Working on assessments – writing critiques and planning essays	9–11 EE reading 10–11 EE lecture 11–12 EE reading 12–1 EE seminar	9–11 Mind reading 11–12 Mind seminar 12–1 Mind lecture	DAY OFF Lie in!	Relax, food shopping, sorting stuff
			L U N C H				
Afternoon 2–6	RA Lecture 2–3 RA Seminar 3–5 ** Library to find and return books etc.	2–3 EE lecture 3–4 Think about 2 lectures, sort notes, consider follow-up 4–5 RA lecture	Shopping, socialising, tidying flat, organising notes, continue writing or catch up on reading if needed	2–4 RA reading and writing critiques 4–6 Mind/ EE reading	Catching up on any work – final burst in library	DAY OFF	Working on assessments – planning and writing essays
			D I N N E R				
Evening 8–11	Write up lecture notes. Decide what to read	Art Society Life Drawing Class	Socialise	Use internet to build up a reading list for assignment	Socialise	DAY OFF	Working on more specific timetable for next week

Figure 2.1

is also trying to keep the focus on one particular subject. The hours you get between timetabled taught sessions can often be frittered away chatting, getting coffee and generally being unfocused. However, if planned carefully they can provide useful reading time, giving you time to relax properly later. Note that by utilising this time before, after and between teaching, 12 hours of reading and thinking can be factored in a week, still leaving plenty of time for writing and research. Katie has also tried to utilise the times she will be more tired – the end of the day – to do the more practical tasks like finding material and photocopying in the library, sorting out notes, and planning what to read next, which help organise the more focused study times. Moreover, by timetabling in the relaxing, social times she is hoping not to become too overwhelmed with work, and also giving herself time to buy and cook good food and keep her study space organised. The discipline of getting up to start work at 9 during the week, should allow her to enjoy her downtime more, keeping on top of her work and appreciating the structure a working week brings. Obviously, this timetable is simply one example of how you could organise your studies. If you are a nightowl who only finds concentration later on in the day, you might want to move the more practical activities to the morning and the reading and writing to the later afternoon and evening. The important thing to remember is that if you get into the habit of working out when you are going to get everything done early on, then you should find it easier to keep on top of your subject, whilst also getting time to socialise and relax.

Make the most of your fellow students as well as the lecturers and support staff

The great thing about studying at university is that there is such a wide range of people for you to work with and learn from. No one does their degree in isolation – no student is an island! So, take advantage and discuss your subject with other students. See if it is useful for you to study together – perhaps helping motivate each other by working for stretches, and then having coffee breaks, or by meeting up to discuss specific readings. Save up questions to ask tutors, and get into the habit of finding people to talk to if you are struggling to keep up, before it gets out of hand.

Develop a system for organising your course material and notes

You will probably feel a bit overloaded with paperwork at the beginning of your degree – and even at the beginning of each module. Much of the material given to you, be it module handbooks, lecture schedules or reading lists may not seem immediately relevant. Similarly, it can be easy to lose

track of your own notes, once you have used them for an assignment – or
to get notes for different subjects mixed together. However, if you develop
a system of keeping all the notes for one subject in a file – or series of files
– and keeping the course information separate from your own notes, then
you should be able to access what you need when you need it. This can save
much time, and also help you keep track of how much information you have
about each section of the module.

● Accessing information

Getting to know the library

The majority of Arts and Humanities subjects will provide you with a reading list at the beginning of each module; it is easy to put off looking at and
thinking about this until the first assignment is due. By this time it is likely
a lot of the useful books will have been borrowed from the library already,
and you won't have much time to undertake the reading you should for
your first essay. It is, therefore, a good idea not only to look at your reading list when you get it, but to begin finding out as soon as you can what
kind of resources the library provides. It can take a bit of time to work out
how to use the library, so it is much better to do this without the pressure
of an imminent deadline hanging over you. Remember: the library staff are
there to help, so whilst it is useful to explore the library yourself and try to
work out its system, it is also worth utilising their expertise and asking them
for guidance; this could save you time in future searches. Many university
libraries provide training for students on arrival – take advantage of these
sessions, they can be a great introduction to the library's many services and
resources. The next section is a brief guide to using the library for research:
it could be used as a checklist to ensure you are taking advantage of everything the library has to offer and learning to research thoroughly.

Searching and browsing

Get used to the idea of both searching for specific books, or specific kinds of
books, and browsing the bookshelves to familiarise yourself with the kind of
material available. The library catalogue will enable you to search for books
by author name, book title, or through a keyword search.

Searching: If you are searching for a specific book from your reading list
put in as much information as possible (it is usually possible to do an author
and title search together) to avoid having to then look through a list of

titles/authors to find the one you need. If you are not looking for a specific book from the reading list, but instead are looking for books about a subject then the keyword search is useful – you may need to experiment with different keyword searches to find a manageable list of book titles you can then look through.

Example of the Search Process

Say you are looking for books on women in the Renaissance period: you might first try a keyword search using 'women' and 'renaissance' as your key words. Leeds University Libraries catalogue gives 206 results for this combined keyword search including books on the Harlem Renaissance and the Italian Renaissance. It may be that you are interested in English Social History, in which case you may decide to add the key word: 'English' to Women and Renaissance – this takes the results down to 68 – a more manageable number. You may then decide you want an even more specific list and also add the words 'social history'. This takes the list down to 7 books – an even more controllable number. You could now go and find these actual books to see which ones look the most useful and accessible.

Browsing: Browsing the shelves in key areas (which you can find, again, through a keyword search), or the recently returned area in your subject, can be a useful way to begin your own investigation of a subject and continue your independent research. Whilst tutors provide reading lists as a guide to the key readings on a subject, they often appreciate students who show evidence they have undertaken research for themselves and gone beyond the reading list.

Good research involves searching *and* browsing – both involve you beginning to think about and engage with the subject. Give yourself time to think: this combination of searching and browsing can enable you to make your own mark on your subject.

TIP
Keep a record of the keyword searches you have done.

Deciding what to do with the books you have found

Once you have found books of interest you need to decide whether to borrow them or to photocopy them; *remember to be realistic about what you are going to read*. It can feel as though you are doing much useful work if you get out lots of books specified on the reading list, or ones you have found which seem relevant, but this becomes a waste of time (and also a heavy burden on your shoulders for no good reason) if you then put them on your shelf, but do not read them.

- Work out how many books you can borrow and for how long – this information should be available on the library webpages; of course, you can always ask library staff as well.
- Take the time in the library to decide what you are going to do with the information you have found. It may be that you decide that some books are so useful you will want to look at them as a whole, whereas others may only really have one pertinent chapter. Photo-copying this chapter – or even reading it there and then and taking notes from it – will allow you space on your library record for other books, as well as space in your room and your bag! In this early stage of library orientation it is best to work out the photocopying system as soon as possible. Most university libraries require you to buy photocopying cards which are available from machines near the photocopiers – if the system is not clear ask one of the library staff. Photocopying usually works out at around 5p a sheet, but if you work out how to do doublesided copies you will halve the cost. I emphasise this, although it may seem obvious, because it can be so useful at an early stage of your university career. Familiarising your-self with how the library works now will save you time and energy later on in your degree when you'll be undertaking large amounts of research for bigger and more complicated assignments.

● The library holds more than books!

So far, I have only been discussing books, but university libraries provide access to a number of other very useful resources. These include:

- journals
- magazines
- electronic resources
- reference books
- manuscripts and archival materials
- databases
- newspapers and microfiche
- dissertations and PhDs.

There is not space to discuss all of these in detail here; at this stage in your academic career, beyond books, the most useful resources for you will be the academic journals in your subject area, together with the databases used for searching them.

● Why use journals?

Journals can be a really good way to find up-to-date information about a subject. This is because, whilst it usually takes years to write a book or compile a collection of essays, most journals come out bi-annually, or even quarterly. Journals are good academic resources because they are peer-reviewed – this means that anything that is published in them has been assessed for quality and accuracy by qualified scholars in the field. This is another reason your tutors like you to use journals as a key resource. Journals, however, can seem less accessible than single-authored books, and textbooks, to students for two main reasons: firstly, you cannot search for journal articles directly on the library catalogue (the catalogue will only tell you where the journal is, not the article in the journal) and secondly, when you find the article you may find that it is about something very specific and written in a complex, seemingly inaccessible way. This is because journals articles are not written to help students write essays – as textbooks often are – they are written to be read by other academics to further the field of research. However, these reasons should not put you off using them. The second issue is dealt with in Chapter 3 – I will deal with the first here.

How to find journal articles

To search for articles in journals you need to become familiar with databases – databases are like large library catalogues which hold information about the articles the journals contain – they enable you to search the contents of many different journals at the same time. Databases tend to be subject-specific, so you may have to become familiar with a number of them to ensure you are searching in all relevant places. You search the database using the same keyword search, or author/title search, you use to search the library catalogue. When you find articles which look relevant you must then find out whether your library holds the journal in which your article is published – this involves doing a journal title search on your library catalogue. If your library has the journal you then need to note down the information from the database about the article which will enable you to find it easily – this will be the author's name, the article title, the volume and issue number of the journal, and the page numbers of the article. Most journals cannot be taken out of the library for more than a day. Skim read the article to see if it will be useful and then photocopy it.

Electronic journals

Many journals available to you via your university library are now accessible online; some databases give you access to the whole journal article which can be downloaded as a PDF. In addition, databases give you the option to read the *abstract*, which can be a good indicator of whether the article will be relevant. Further, the database may provide information about related articles, or those which have cited your article; this can be a useful way to continue your research.

The journal article hunt

Find a database which deals with your subject – library staff or your tutors should be able to help you with this if you are struggling.

1 Perform a keyword search – keep a record of the keyword searches you have done.

2 Assess the number of results that this search has produced: do you have far too many articles to search through? If so, try to make the search more specific – perhaps by adding more words. On the other hand, perhaps your search did not really give you anything useful, or anything at all? If so, widen your search or try another word. Experiment with the database's advanced search options – it may be useful to limit the dates, or specify the language.

3 Once the list is at a manageable size, look through it and note down which articles you want to go and find. Some databases might give you access to the abstracts – in which case skim through these when assessing whether an article could be useful. Some might link to the whole article – in which case you can download the ones that seem useful straightaway. Some might provide links at the side to articles related to the one you are looking at – take a look at this to see if it suggests anything useful.

4   If you have found articles you want to read but they are not available to download, then follow the database checklist below and see if the article is available for you in the library. If you have found nothing – try changing databases, as long as you are sure you have covered all likely keyword searches with this one.

5   When you have access to the journal articles which seem useful, skim read them before printing them off/photocopying them. Realising later that something is not useful is a waste of time and paper.

Database checklist

What information do I need when looking for a journal article?

Once you have found an intriguing and relevant-looking article title on a database the search does not end there. You next need to see if the article is in the library. For this you will need the following information, in this order:

- Journal title (you will first search for this on the library catalogue, as you would search for a book)
- Volume number AND issue number – usually written like this: 4.2
- Date
- Page numbers
- Article title
- Article author

> **TIP**
> Research breeds research. Once you have found one useful journal article, look in the reference list and you should find many more. Each article is a resource in itself.

● Using the internet for research

The internet can be a very useful research tool, for non-scholars and scholars. It must, however, be treated with caution – this cannot be emphasised enough. Most of the resources available to you in the library have been assessed independently to ensure they are accurate, and of sufficient quality and integrity. Websites, on the other hand, can be set up by anyone, with any level of expertise, and with any level of integrity. This does not mean you cannot trust *any* of the information you find on the internet – but it does mean you need to develop your own ways of assessing (a) what information is trustworthy and (b) how you should use the information you find. Here are some top tips for approaching internet research.

Always be critical when searching the web

Remember to appraise information and assess its quality. Ask yourself what you want from a resource. How can you make sure it will give you the quality of information needed for a critical academic essay?

> **Author?** What are the author's credentials and affiliation? Is there any e-mail contact information? Has any vested interest, sponsorship been disclosed? Which companies or funding bodies are behind the resource?
> **Content?** Is it accurate, up-to-date? Are links regularly maintained? When was the page last modified? Is there user support?
> **Context?** Is it relevant? Who is the target audience? As a public domain service the internet's potential audience lacks focus and is heterogeneous. When you review a resource ask yourself the basic question: is this aimed at me as an academic researcher?
> **Authority?** What level of authority does it have? Is it hosted by a parent organisation? Does it have its own domain name? The URL (address of the website) can disclose important information about the nature of a site. Go for legitimate sites: universities, academic organizations and ones recommended by subject gateways such as *Intute* <http://www.intute.ac.uk>
> **Attribution?** Is there any reference source data, links to that data or evidence to support any claims that are made?
> **Stability?** Is it a durable resource? Is it also published in print format? Is it accessible, quick to access?

> **EXERCISE** Evaluating internet resources
>
> Look at the extracts from three different websites – and if possible, look at the websites too. Think about how appropriate they would be as research resources for an academic essay on Darwinism. Consider:
>
> - Who their intended audience is.
> - The tone of the site.
> - Where they are getting their information from (for example, to what extent is the information on the website referenced?).
>
> Once you have taken into account these three factors, rank them: how appropriate are they for using as sources for your academic essay? List the reasons for your decision. Compare your thoughts to ours on page 184 at the back of the book.
>
> *Website 1* Wikipedia, 'Darwinism' http://en.wikipedia.org/wiki/Darwinism [Accessed, 22.09.2008]

Darwinism is a term used for various different movements or concepts related to a greater or lesser extent to Charles Darwin's work on evolution.[1] The meaning of *Darwinism* has changed over time, and depends on who is using the term.[2]

The term was coined by Thomas Henry Huxley in April 1860,[3] and was used to describe evolutionary concepts, including earlier concepts such as Malthusianism and Spencerism. In the late 19th century it came to mean the concept that natural selection was the sole mechanism of evolution, in contrast to Lamarckism, then around 1900 it was eclipsed by Mendelism until the modern evolutionary synthesis unified Darwin's and Gregor Mendel's ideas. As modern evolutionary theory has developed, the term has been associated at times with specific ideas.[2]

While the term has remained in use amongst scientific authors, it is increasingly regarded as an inappropriate description of modern evolutionary theory.[4][5][6] For example, Darwin was unfamiliar with the work of Gregor Mendel, having as a result only a vague and inaccurate understanding of heredity, although he had an unopened copy of Mendel's works in his library (see Pangenesis), and knew nothing of genetic drift.[7] In modern usage, particularly in the United States, *Darwinism* is often used by creationists as a pejorative term.[8]

Website 2   Donald deMarco, 'Faith in the Age of Science', *Catholic. Net,* http://catholic.net/index.php?option=dedestaca&origen=3&id= 645 [Accessed 23.9.2008]

Charles Darwin, Sigmund Freud and Karl Marx all believed that they had given the world a scientific blueprint for better living. Yet their theories, though proclaimed as scientific, are replete with errors and half-truths, and have brought about the nightmares of social Darwinism that opposes altruism, Freudian psychology that suppresses the spirit, and a Marxist socialism that negates both love and spirituality.

Science cannot provide a path to personal holiness. Its purview is much too small for that. But faith is of a different order, and one that can unite us with God.

It is also a grave mistake to reduce faith to mere subjectivity. Prayer, properly understood, is not a soliloquy but a communion. It does not lack an object in truth, since it is linked with God. Good works unite us with our neighbor as well as with God.

There is a reverse side to our present age of science that is aptly described as the Age of Anxiety. Playwright Arthur Miller refers to the modern world as "an air-conditioned nightmare."

Why? Because science without faith makes us cosmic orphans, and we shudder in fear when we are cognizant of our own littleness and our utter helplessness in the face of death.

Faith in science is misplaced faith. Faith in God, in Christ, nourished through prayer and good works (as well as the sacraments), is what we need as the most viable means of finding truth and fulfilling our destinies as human beings.

Donald DeMarco is adjunct professor at Holy Apostles College and Seminary in Cromwell, Connecticut.

Make a Donation Now!
Your support for Catholic.net helps to build a culture of life in our nation and throughout the world. Please help us promote the Church's new evangelization by donating to Catholic.net right now. God bless you for your generosity.

Exercise continued

Website 3   Robert M. Young, 'Darwin's Metaphor: Does Nature Select?', Human-Nature.com, http://human-nature.com/dm/chap4.html [Accessed 23.9.2008]

It is not too great an exaggeration to claim that *On the Origin of Species* was, along with *Das Kapital*, one of the two most significant works in the intellectual history of the nineteenth century. As George Henry Lewes wrote in 1868, "No work of our time has been so general in its influence." However, the very generality of the influence of Darwin's work provides the chief problem for the intellectual historian. Most books and articles on the subject assert the influence but remain very imprecise about its nature. It is very difficult indeed to assess what it was about the Darwinian theory which was so influential and how its influence was felt. This problem in Victorian intellectual history intersects with a related one in the history of science. There has been a tendency on the part of historians of science to isolate Darwin in two related ways. The first is to single him out from the mainstream of nineteenth-century naturalism in Britain and allow "Darwinism" to stand duty for the wider movement of which it was in fact but a part. The second is the tendency to single out his evolutionary theory and to demarcate it sharply from those of his predecessors and contemporaries. According to this interpretation Darwin stood alone as a real, empirical scientist and provided the first genuinely scientific hypothesis for the process by which evolution might have occurred. The theories of the other main evolutionists – Erasmus Darwin, Lamarck, Chambers, Spencer, and Wallace – were more or less besmirched by ideological, anthropomorphic, or other "nonscientific" factors or by the uses to which they were put by their authors. Charles Darwin is thus made to stand out as a figure of comparatively unalloyed scientific status and is treated in relative isolation from the social and intellectual context in which he worked and into which his theory was received.

Compare your thoughts to ours on page 184 at the back of the book.

● Making the most of your contact time

What is the best way to approach lecture-based teaching?

A lecture is designed as a way to deliver information; unlike seminars and tutorials, lectures are not usually interactive. Rather, they involve listening to an argument presented by the lecturer. This does not mean, however, that you should expect lectures to be a passive experience; they are not really intended to be an opportunity for you to relax, sit back and listen without thinking about what is being said. In fact, if you attempt to treat lectures like this you will find yourself unable to take in the information you are receiving and will most likely get restless and bored. Because lecturers have a certain amount of information to convey lectures cannot always be as entertaining as you might want; further, it is difficult for anyone to concentrate on listening to anything for as long as an hour. This all means that you have to go to lectures as prepared as possible; the key is that you should *already be thinking about the subject*. Go to a lecture without any idea of what it might be about, and you will most likely spend the first 10 minutes or so disoriented and trying to work out what is going on. Go to a lecture prepared, having in mind what the lecturer will be talking about and why, and you will already have some context for what the lecturer is saying and will be able to get to grips with the subject-matter from the start.

There are different kinds of lectures

Something important to bear in mind when considering how to approach lectures is that different lectures aim for different effects. If you can develop a flexible approach to lectures, you should find them more comprehensible, and more useful. For example, some lectures will aim to give you a broad background of a subject, some will give you an example of a very specific argument about a topic, and some will give you more direct guidelines about how you can direct your own thinking. Many lectures, of course, will aim for a combination of these effects. But you should not expect all lectures to do so; and you should certainly not see lectures as a substitute for your own independent research. They can be understood as a jumping-off point to your own thinking and as an opportunity for you to think through ideas. They are *not* there to provide everything there is to know about a subject and they should present as many questions as they provide answers.

Preparing for lectures

So, having said all this, what is the best way to prepare for lectures? Make sure you know as far as possible what they are going to discuss by:

- Consulting course materials which should provide you with a course outline, and a mini summary of what each lecture will aim to do. At the very least it will give you a title for the lecture.
- Making sure you remember what happened in the last lecture – it is good practice to skim through the previous lecture notes before you attend the next lecture. This way the module issues are clear in your mind and any connections which can be made between the ideas in the lectures will jump out for you more easily.
- Finishing any set texts under discussion. You will follow a lecture with more ease and interest if you are familiar with the material under discussion; you could use your module reading list to give you ideas about what to read in preparation for the lecture.
- Thinking about what kind of questions you want answering from the lecture or what kinds of critical approaches or readings might be made. (This will mean you are listening *for* something.)

Listening effectively in lectures

Having prepared for the lecture, there are strategies you can employ in the lecture to ensure you follow as much as possible of what is being said. The challenge is to pick out the main points so you can think about them afterwards. Try to remember that it is virtually impossible to remember everything that is said in a lecture, and that no two people get the same information from a lecture. You are aiming to engage with the lecture in your own way, and get the information which is of interest and use to you. In order to do this:

- Make notes about the *main* points (you really should not try to write everything down).
- Think about how the lecturer is structuring their argument. (This can give you an idea of how to structure your own arguments in essays, as well as help you follow what they are saying.)
- Make sure you take notice of any useful references – and keep notes about your own ideas that have been provoked in the lecture.

- make good use of any handouts provided. It can be easier to take notes on the handout, which will often give a skeleton structure of the lecturer's argument.

Follow-up activities after the lecture

Just as it is important to prepare for a lecture, ideally you should be giving yourself time to think about it afterwards. Often you will have a seminar which will give you an opportunity to discuss the subject. This may not always happen, however, and even if it does it is also useful to make sure you have given yourself a chance to consolidate the information received and develop your own stance about it. (For more information see **Developing your Critical Voice** in Chapter 4 (p. 82).) Suggestions for follow-up activities are:

- Go over your notes whilst the lecture is still fresh in your mind and clarify any unclear passages.
- Identify any areas you did not understand which you could then research for yourself further.
- Ask the lecturer (or fellow students) for clarification on any unclear points – all lecturers should have office hours designed, in part, for this purpose.
- Think about how the lecture connects to the course as a whole, and how it could help with the assessed parts of the course and your seminar discussions.
- Make sure you end up with a set of lecture notes which make clear what you have learnt and what you can do with that information. You'll be able to refer back to these easily when undertaking assignments or revising. This set of notes could contain references to further reading, or could even be filed together with further reading you have done on the subject.
- Make a note for yourself about whether any PowerPoint™ slides from the lecture will be available for you to look at – make sure you note where these can be found for future reference.
- Give yourself the opportunity to talk lectures through with fellow students.

Here is an example of some lecture notes, to give you an idea of how they can be laid out to contain the main points, and highlight particular areas you need to follow up in your own learning.

24/10/09
French autobiography Lecture 1

<u>Why are writers drawn to autobiography?</u>
- To achieve sthg; to learn sthg about self (La Bâtarde)
- To achieve understanding, absolution, forgiveness from reader
- To instruct or impress the reader (Sartre, Gide, Beauvoir)
- To elicit form of love from reader (Leduc)
- To ward off effect of aging (Beauvoir)

Authors have diff. emotional involvement in autob. than fiction.
More complex reasons
- Lack. Freud and Lacan have suggested that human subject has
  no core single entity with an 'essence' or 'wholeness'
  ⇨ autob. allows writer to define self, give self shape. Autob.,
  then, is v. reassuring (not to describe ourselves but to
  <u>construct</u> a self) — see 'Qui est-ce ce Violette Leduc?' See
  quote 3 handout 1.
  We have a gap and writing makes us whole.
  One stage further, see quote 4, we see life as chaotic and
  arbitrary and Autob. gives it shape and direction. — Autob.
  as THERAPY. driven by a "will to form" (M. Sheringham), to
  make life ordered + meaningful. Impose order of present on
  chaos of past.
- Duty. Feeling of having to constitute moral lesson about being —
  often set self up as negative example (Sartre, Sachs — Beauvoir
  sets self up as positive but for same reason)
- To write the 'great work'. For people who've already reached
  the pinnacle of career, this is a final gesture. Should be well-
  known B4 writing Autob.

<u>What does the genre claim to achieve?</u> (classic autoB.)
- It's a referential narrative form (relates to the real): the 1st
  message we receive is that <u>reality</u> of the past life is captured in
  the text.
- It's telling the 'truth' about its subject
- The story it offers is a sincere story.

These 3 messages are v. problematic + flawed because:-
- The autoB. will always be selective (Beauvoir attempts to mask
  this but necessarily fails)

- An author can't know the truth about himself. Aspects of his past won't be transparent to him.
- When author chooses to write a self-portrait, the facts will be chosen to create a particular self-image (Beauvoir, Sartre)

Subject bent   subject living
on freedom   in bad faith

****So Autob. will always be PARTIAL, in both senses of the word. Subject of AutoB. narrative will never coincide completely with the writing subject, ref quote 5: the present author bears on conception of younger subject: the author wants to be seen in a certain way: both a referential, real subject, and a narrative creation.

PLUS, language cannot tell the truth. Quote 6. Words have a tangential relation to the real. Language evolves, meaning changes with time. As autoB. is a linguistic artefact, it cannot be true. BUT, if autoB. doesn't tell THE truth, it does tell A truth. Not objective, not total — it's partial + biased but is nonetheless a truth that the author wants to embrace. At the least, autoB. tells us sthg about autobiographer at time of writing.
Most authors DO NOT claim to offer the whole truth.

Note:
- **underlining** to signify the different sections of the lecture (and so structure of the argument), AND to signify the titles of books.
- **bullet points** used as an efficient means to list ideas and examples.
- **abbreviations** which can be easily understood afterwards (sthg = something, autoB = autobiography).
- **brackets** to expand and give examples to think about afterwards (the brackets usually contain names of authors or books).
- the **connection** made between some ideas and quotations on the hand-out – so when notes are looked at again, these connections can be thought about.
- **stars** (***) to indicate a key point.
- **visual aids** such as arrows to indicate flow of argument, capital letters to emphasise particularly important words, and highlighting to signify important concepts.

Consider also that these are notes from a one-hour lecture – so might seem quite brief. The student has put down the main points, and kept the structure of the argument – rather than trying to write down everything. By noting down examples, and referring to the handout, she has given herself a chance to think about what has been said later, and so remember and follow up what she has learnt.

> **Top Tip**
> Although this might all seem a lot of work for each lecture, if it is worked into your routine, it will not seem like much at all. You should only need 20 mins at most to make your notes clear and think about what other follow-up is needed. This 20 mins could save you so much more time when you are addressing the issues of the lecture in essay or exam preparation later.

Preparing for seminars

As well as lectures, you'll also be attending classes in which you will be expected to interact: these are usually referred to as either seminars or tutorials. They provide an opportunity for you to sharpen your **critical thinking** about a subject and so help you develop the analytical skills which are tested through examination and written assignments. Seminars and tutorials are designed to help you develop your ideas and knowledge about the module by:

- Giving you the opportunity to test out your ideas with other people.
- Giving you the space to ask questions about the course.
- Helping you make contacts with fellow students to discuss issues in your own time.

To get the most out of these sessions you need to **prepare carefully** which might involve:

- Making sure you have read and *understood* the set text, or, if there are parts that you don't understand, that you come prepared with questions about these.
- Becoming acquainted with secondary material on the subject: this will not only give you something additional to discuss but will broaden your critical and conceptual understanding of set texts.
- Undertaking any tasks/exercises set by your tutor.

- Writing out a list of points/questions you think it might be useful to raise in the session.
- Beginning to discuss issues with fellow students *before* the session.

In the seminar

- Try to follow the discussion by listening carefully and contributing. Don't take excessive notes: if you spend the whole time taking notes you will not have given yourself the opportunity to ask questions, make comments and appreciate the variety of opinions around the room.
- Try to listen to and talk to your fellow students. In larger group discussions a lot of students address their remarks to the tutor only; this can prevent a discussion from really happening. What happens instead is a stilted situation – one in which the tutor asks a question, someone answers and then the tutor asks another – rather than a more fluid and satisfying discussion that can happen if students respond to each other's ideas without being prompted.
- Ask questions if you are not following what is happening. Sometimes the tutor will phrase a question in a way that is difficult to understand. If this happens, asking them to rephrase what they have said is a good strategy, and will often be appreciated by tutors who are not sure why there is a silence.

After the seminar

- Write up any ideas from the seminar you think will be important or you want to follow up.
- Think of the ways in which the discussion in the seminar continued/ differed from the ideas in the lecture.
- Think about how the seminar discussion fits into your learning on the module as a whole.

Presentations in seminars

It is very likely you will be asked to do a presentation to introduce a seminar or present ideas on a specific subject. Sometimes you may be asked to work with someone else. Tutors use presentations to give you the opportunity to present your ideas in a more formal way to your fellow students, and to give you the chance to get more immediate feedback on those ideas from the other students and the tutor. They are an opportunity to show you have something interesting to say on the subject at hand and, if you are less confident in contributing in seminars, to contribute on something you have prepared beforehand.

So, what makes a good presentation? Preparation should help ensure that you feel confident to talk about a subject – but this should not necessarily involve spending hours writing out a script to read out. Listening to someone read something out is rarely easy and can be pretty boring, however interesting the ideas. You want your presentation to stand out as well thought-through and interesting. It is, therefore, good if you can have a set of notes to aid your talk, rather than a script. This could help you talk to your fellow students, rather than read something out monotonously.

It is also important to demonstrate a critical engagement with the subject. This involves showing you have understood the main issues, reflected upon them and produced your own analyses. For example, in English literature many students spend valuable presentation time talking about the author's biography when they could be analysing their work, close reading examples about which the other students could be developing their own ideas.

Suggested techniques for remaining calm

Talking in front of people can be daunting. You may find the following suggestions helpful if you find the idea of doing a presentation stressful:

- Practise in front of people first – these could be fellow students, or even family members or friends.
- It can be a good idea to provide handouts as something for your audience to focus on – this also easily demonstrates that you have planned and organised your thoughts.
- Make sure you have all visual material ready and sorted out, so you are not worried about that whilst talking.
- Avoid coffee beforehand – this just increases the jitters. Drink water or herbal tea and breathe deeply.
- When giving the presentation don't catch anyone's eye if this makes you nervous – find a spot in your sightline that you can look at when thinking about your next point.
- Don't speak too fast – try to take it one idea at a time.
- If there are aspects of the presentation you are worried about, arrange to talk to the tutor about them.

> Learning how to do oral presentations is a good transferable skill – so try and treat them as an opportunity to practise expressing your ideas and getting immediate feedback.

One-to-one sessions with your tutor

All university departments should give you the opportunity to talk to a tutor one-to-one. Take advantage of this and use these meetings wisely. All tutors have Consultation hours which are also referred to as Office, or Surgery, hours. Look at your tutor's door for times, or ask at the School or Department's General Office. This information should also be available in the module documentation provided by your module tutor. Consultation hours are set aside for you to discuss your concerns about a course, a module, an essay or any question relating to your academic study. For example you may want to:

- Discuss what is expected of an assignment.
- Check you are on the right track with an assignment.
- Talk about a discussion you did not understand or want to take further from a class.
- Comment on the way classes or lectures are going.

You may find it useful to write the issues down that you want to discuss, or email your tutor beforehand, to make sure you get what you need from the meeting.

Summary

Learning how to be a student is a process – and involves getting to grips with many different kinds of tasks and challenges. This chapter has discussed some general ways in which you can get organised and become prepared – as well as going through some more specific ways you can approach research and university teaching. Our key advice is to try and start *enjoying* studying, learning and researching: this is a time that new ideas and theories will open up to you and become real and intellectually exciting. You are now a member of a wider academic community: now is the time to enter the debate in your subject area and make a contribution to your discipline – through reading, writing, listening, researching and talking. Good luck!

3 Effective Reading: A Vital Part of the Writing Process

● Introduction to reading at university

Pretty early on in your time at university your tutors will emphasise that it is their job to help you begin taking charge of your own studies; in other words, the lecturers are not there to tell you what to think – they will guide you through your own independent learning. Reading will form the biggest part of this learning, and as such you need to get used to dedicating a lot of your time to it. In addition, you may find that the reading techniques and note-making strategies you developed at school are not so useful in a university environment. Bear in mind that you have never had to read before in a higher education context, so you will probably find some of the reading difficult, as well as finding that the amount you need to read in a short space of time has gone up dramatically from what you have found previously. This chapter is designed to help you think about the different kinds of reading you will have to do at university, as well as consider ways in which you can improve your own reading and note-making strategies.

> At university you will use reading to fill in your knowledge gaps, find out what a range of specialists have said about a subject, widen your understanding and expand your horizons. Taking reading seriously at the beginning of your degree is vital if you are to follow, enjoy and succeed at a subject.

Reading is not simply comprehension

The word 'reading' refers both to the activity of 'reproducing mentally or vocally written or printed words', and 'deducing or declaring an interpretation' of the written word. It can also refer to the act of interpretation generally – for example a metereologist reads the sky for signs of weather change, a card player reads her hand to decide how to play, a detective reads between the lines to solve the case. The dictionary tells us that the word 'read' comes from the Old English (originally from the Germanic) to 'advise, consider, discern' – and it is worth bearing this broad definition in mind when approaching your reading tasks at university. The diverse range of material you will come across will become much more interesting if you approach it thinking you will be discerning meaning, but then through a considered interpretation, advising others of the most important points of the material, thinking also about the way you will be using the material, and reading between the lines to develop your own argument. To achieve this kind of reading you need to dedicate time to looking at the text and discerning the meaning, but also to contemplating the various ways it could be interpreted. Considering reading in this way should also help make you aware you are reading all the time and your reading skills are becoming more sophisticated with every new experience. We read people when we meet them, you will read – in the sense of interpret – lectures, and visual material such as paintings and films for meaning. To think of it as reading is, I think, to acknowledge the work that goes into the interpretation – reading involves continual consideration and contemplation, it means keeping your mind open, asking questions and making interpretations.

● What kind of texts will I be reading?

During your university life you will read many different genres of writing and will learn to distinguish between diverse agendas whilst being aware of your own. For example, a history student will not only read historical text-books, but will also most likely read such source material as newspapers, census data and political documents; each of these writings require a different kind of reading. A philosophy student will be expected to read the work of a variety of philosophers; each will have their own challenging style of writing. In addition, the philosophy student will have to read the critics and followers of these philosophers.

My point is that whatever subject you are undertaking you need to develop as a flexible reader who can respond to the different kinds of writing with which you will be asked to engage. Furthermore, you yourself will be reading for a variety of reasons often with a changing agenda. Sometimes you will be reading to gain background knowledge for a lecture or seminar, sometimes you will be researching for a specific essay, sometimes you will be following up the ideas presented in a discussion. Each of these modes of reading requires a different skill and technique to be effective. This chapter aims to help you hone these techniques and develop your reading skills by making you aware of different strategies you can use to approach the diverse and challenging texts your degree will introduce you to.

What will you be reading?

Theory and philosophy

All Arts and Humanities subjects will involve the consideration of a range of key theoretical and critical concepts. In your degree you will need to find ways to understand these by reading about them and then discussing and applying them to various cultural products and situations. The exciting thing for you, the student, is that you are expected to have your own ideas and opinions about the key concepts and ideas. You can develop these opinions and ideas through reading about them in a variety of ways:

- You will be asked to consider the writings of the theorists/ philosophers themselves – looking at what their ideas are and how they present them. This kind of reading is often challenging because the theorists are not writing to be easily accessible, often expressing their complex ideas in dense texts. The benefit of this kind of reading, however, is that it allows you to begin to understand what the theorist is really saying and have your own opinion about it, rather than relying on someone else's interpretation.
- You will find it helpful to consult guidance material from various sources which provides explanation and interpretation about the work of the theorist. Often this material is recommended on the reading lists the tutor provides, and it can be a useful way to begin to see how others have understood and used the theorist's work, giving you a place to develop your own reading.
- It is also useful to read examples of the way the theory is used – thinking about how effective it is in application.

Fictional/Artistic works (novels, poetry, drama etc ...)

Many Arts and Humanities degrees train you to become sophisticated readers of different creative texts, about which you will develop your own interpretation of what is presented and how it is presented – by reading carefully. You will also be required to be both sensitive to the situation in which these texts were produced and aware of the context in which you are reading them.

- You will be asked to consider the creative work itself; forming your own readings of the set texts on the module

- In addition, you will need to consider other writers' opinions of the work and use this as one approach to developing your perception of it.
- Further, it would be useful for you to think about the place of the particular set texts in relation to other creative works, both by the same writer and by other writers who are contemporary *and* from different time periods.

Historical documents and source material

In the course of your research you may be asked to draw upon material from the particular time and place you are writing about – this could be man- uscripts from the nineteenth century, fashion magazines from the 1980s, German newspapers from the second world war, the book from an art exhi- bition, interviews. With this material you need to:

- Try to keep in mind what you are trying to get from it, and what it is telling you about the context you are researching.
- It is also useful to think about how the source you are looking at compares to others.
- Remember that looking at source material gives you a chance to make your own assessment of a situation so dedicate the time to reading it carefully and reaching your own conclusions.

Secondary material

To give you a context for the theoretical, creative and source material you will find yourself consulting a lot of secondary material – material written about the theory/cultural product/source. This secondary material will allow you to become part of a bigger conversation about your topic, giving you an idea of how others have discussed it. It will present you with opin- ions and interpretations of the topic you are researching but you should not use it as a substitute for your own thinking. It is there for you to:

1. Treat critically.
2. Use in your own discussion judiciously.
3. Respond to thoughtfully.

Websites and other internet resources

For many students, who increasingly have access to the internet at home as well as at university, the internet may be the most accessible place to begin research. It can provide a wealth of information about whatever subject you are researching – for most topics you will probably be able to access many seemingly relevant websites very quickly. The tricky thing then becomes sifting out what is going to be useful – the exercise in Chapter 2 (p. 28) is designed to help you think about this. Suffice to say here that you need to:

● Approach the internet with a critical mind; the first site you come across from a search is rarely the most useful – allow the time to find the most relevant.
● As with sources, think about the agenda behind a site and how it could be useful in providing context for your research.
● Keep track of what information you have got from which site – for your own records (so you know what you have looked at) and to make sure you reference correctly and do not accidentally plagiarise.

> Whatever you are reading – keep an open mind, read between the lines, and make a note of the ideas and interpretations you have whilst contemplating.

● Coping with module reading lists

Reading lists are provided by tutors for a variety of reasons which can be split into four main categories:

1. To let you know the required reading for the module.
2. To give you an idea of the kind of background reading you should be undertaking to understand lectures, participate in seminars and complete assignments.
3. To suggest preparatory texts to introduce you to key ideas and concepts on the module.
4. To give you an idea of extra reading you could undertake to take your ideas further.

Dealing with long reading lists

Reading lists can often seem long and intimidating and it can be tempting to ignore them altogether if you are not given an indication of where to start.

Firstly, you should work out, perhaps by asking your tutor or looking for an indication on the reading list, what the list is aiming to do, as well as considering how you are going to use it.

If it is a preparatory reading list, then take a look at the choice of books on offer and perhaps pick two to consider in detail, if it is a background reading list see which books are available and perhaps aim to read something from this reading list as well as the required reading every week. This way you will build up a good range of background knowledge which you can draw upon when preparing for written assignments, examinations and seminars.

If you are really struggling to decide what to read from the reading list, it could be helpful to ask your tutor to help you narrow it down. Bear in mind, however, that they may already feel they have narrowed it down enough by providing the list in the first place. In this case, try going to the library to browse some of the books suggested to see what interests you and looks most useful. Also, your fellow students might be able to advise you on useful articles and books they have read.

Dealing with sparse reading lists

It may be that the reading list you have received for the module seems very short and not comprehensive enough. This may be because your tutor only considers a few texts to be vital reading for the module; it may be because they are encouraging you to find useful, interesting texts to provide a background and context for your learning yourself. In this case, try to ensure you do access the reading recommended, whilst undertaking your own research, perhaps checking with your tutor that you are on the right track with the texts you find before spending a lot of time reading them.

Getting hold of the books on the reading list

Some reading lists provide you with library classmarks, some don't and it is your job to look them up on the library catalogue. If you have any difficulties finding material on the reading list, there are people in every university library trained and happy to help. Some guidelines are also provided in the *research* section of Chapter 2 (pp. 23–5). I cannot stress enough the importance of finding materials on the reading list as soon as possible; the later you leave it, the more likely it is other students will have taken out the recommended texts. It is a good idea to be really prepared and photocopy some of the recommended reading before you will need it, so it will be there ready in good time. If you do not want to risk photocopying material you will not need, it is still a good idea to get an idea of what kind of reading you will be required to engage with by browsing recommended books at an early stage. If you do go to the library and find that everything on the reading list has been taken out remember three things:

1. Most university libraries allow you to reserve books which are already checked out. This will usually mean that the book should be returned within a week.
2. Most reading lists are not comprehensive so you can use your initiative and search for useful material beyond the reading list.
3. An increasing amount of useful research material is being put online, so make sure you know how to access useful online journals and databases. See the library section of Chapter 2 (p. 25) for more information about this.

> **Remember**   Start reading early. Keep track of what you have read, both the ideas of others, your own interpretations of these and the full reference details of any book you have taken notes from, and start to identify particular areas of interest, thinking about the way your ideas are developing through the contemplation of each text.

● Reading as part of the writing process

Being an Arts and Humanities student at university means developing as a critical thinker; reading and writing are the skills you will need to become a more sophisticated analyser of the world, giving you many different ways of thinking about it. You will mainly be assessed through written assignments, examinations and oral presentations. Whilst your actual written and presentation skills will be the elements of your work directly submitted for assessment, it is your reading skills which will most profoundly improve your work and which your tutors are both aiming to improve and assess. So, you need to start thinking about reading as a fundamental part of the writing process. Not only is it through reading that you find information about a subject, reading is also necessary as a way of understanding how different scholars have approached and assessed a topic and is vital for helping you formulate your own views.

Reading is part of the writing process. You will need to:

● Dedicate a substantial portion of time to it in your weekly study timetable.

- Realise the importance of developing strategies you can use to make sure you *not only* remember and can utilise what you have read, but have also considered how you are going to use it as part of your seminar/assignment discussion.
- Read *actively*. This involves *doing* something with the text you are reading rather than trying to passively absorb it. Active approaches will be suggested later in this chapter; these are designed to help you become more efficient at both understanding and critically responding to texts.

Finally, reading can help you learn to write: you can use the writing of others to help improve your own writing and research techniques, and by this I mean two things. Take a critical text as an example: firstly, as well as reading for the content of someone's argument, think about how it is structured, what evidence they are using, etc., and secondly, look at their references and bibliography, are there any texts they have cited that could be useful for you to read?

Incorporating reading into your study schedule

Having outlined the need to consider reading as part of the writing process, I now want to emphasise the significant amount of time you should dedicate to it weekly. The reading you are going to be asked to do at university will not always be the most accessible, so it will almost always be difficult, and sometimes counterproductive, to try to tackle it at the last minute. It would be good, then, to get used to developing an action plan to make sure you get the required and useful extra reading done at a pace productive for you. Your degree will require you to spend much of your time reading, but it is important to consider, also, that whilst this sounds monotonous, different kinds of texts and so different kinds of reading will be involved at different times; so, you need to set aside times of the day conducive to each kind of reading.

Top tips for keeping on top of your reading

Routine

Set aside significant time each week to read regularly; you will get better and more confident about the variety of complex texts your degree involves the more frequently you do it. Getting into a routine is a good idea, especially if you have large difficult texts to tackle. For example, if you find you concentrate best and are the most awake in the morning then reserve the morning times not taken up with teaching for the most difficult reading tasks of the week.

Tackle bite-sized chunks

If you have a difficult chunk of text to read adjust your expectations; it will take longer, so split it up into bite-sized chunks and take small breaks between each one, making sure you have understood what you have read.

Select

If you really are pushed for time, try to work out the most important parts of a text you will need to read, or within the breaks of a more difficult text read easier, more accessible texts to aid your understanding. This is a good example of active reading, a term which incorporates a whole host of strategies which involve you doing something *with* the reading. I outline these in the Reading Strategies section of this chapter.

Adapt

Allow different amounts of time for different kinds of reading. A dense philosophical text will need to be read carefully and slowly at a time your concentration is the best whilst a textbook may be skimmed through quickly.

Keep track of your understanding

Don't waste time pursuing a text you really do not understand at all. If you are having real trouble try to find a guide to the text you are reading, or something more accessible; if you have trouble with this ask a tutor or fellow student for help and advice.

Find a good study space

Make sure you have found a place where you can concentrate. For many people it is more difficult to concentrate on reading than it is on writing as it is potentially a more passive activity, more out of your control. Therefore, it is very important to try and find somewhere you will be least bothered by distractions. The top floor of a library, first thing in the morning is a good example of somewhere likely to be quiet. Also, this might sound silly, but anywhere too warm and comfortable may be tempting but is dangerous, because it is the place you are most likely to fall asleep. Ideally you want to find somewhere quiet, tidy, with good light (so you don't strain your eyes), and with desk space so you can take notes.

● Reading strategies

Reading can potentially be quite a passive activity, and it can seem dull, monotonous, and be difficult to concentrate on. This means you will need to find ways to increase your engagement with and concentration on the text. This involves *doing* something with the text rather than simply trying to read it passively. Table 3.1 shows the differences between active and passive reading.

Passive	Active
Inefficient – often leads to having to read the same text a number of times	Keeps your concentration going, meaning you get more from the text the first time
Reading a text from beginning to end	Always being clear about why you are reading, and what you are looking for
Reading unquestioningly, taking it one sentence at a time	Reading interrogatively, keeping track of what you are getting from a text
Not thinking about why you are reading, or what you want to get from the text	Keeping a record of your own responses

Looking for the sections of the text which will be most useful for you |

Table 3.1   Passive vs active reading

Targeted reading is a version of active reading, and simply involves approaching a text having decided what specific things you need to get from it and how you are going to use it. The following section describes some active and targeted approaches to thinking about different reading issues and strategies.

● Reading process

Figure 3.1 shows the four stages of the reading process.

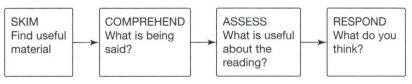

Figure 3.1   The reading process

Skim reading: finding what you want from your texts

Skim reading can be risky if you don't have a focus; it implies reading fast, but can often result in you not really reading anything at all *if* you do not have a strategy for how it is going to work. As with all reading you need to work out what you are hoping to get out of the reading. If reading for an assignment or for seminar preparation doublecheck before you begin what the specific requirements are; if reading for your own wider comprehension of the subject, it is useful to list beforehand what you do know about the subject and what you are trying to find out from this reading. Skim reading can then help you decide whether the text you are looking at will potentially be useful for you.

Skim reading strategies

Contents and index pages

Take advantage of the way books are structured. Most books have a contents page and an index. Firstly, use the contents page to see what the book is focusing on and where, noting the chapters which look the most relevant. If there is something very specific you are researching which is not mentioned in the contents page, look in the index in the back of the book to see if it is mentioned there, and if so how frequently. If it isn't mentioned this does not necessarily mean this subject is not dealt with. It is worth remembering that different indexes have different priorities so whilst you may be looking for a particular topic the index may only list it under the authors' names OR may mention the topic but use a different word. Allow time to spend browsing the index, then, as this could save you the time you may have spent trying to browse the book as a whole, or taking out books which are not useful.

Structure of chapter/article

When establishing what a chapter or article is about, it is again worth taking advantage of the way it is structured.

Abstract

Chapters in textbooks, as well as some articles, often begin with an abstract, which consists of one or two paragraphs summarising what the whole piece of writing is about. Since this is a summary, it is worth reading carefully as this should not only let you know whether the piece will be useful to you, but it will also give you an idea of direction of the writer's argument, which will make it easier to follow if you do decide to read the whole thing.

Introduction and conclusion

Even if the article/chapter doesn't have an abstract it will have an introduction which will be designed to outline what the piece of writing will be about and how it is structured. Similarly, the conclusion should sum up the main points, and emphasise the most important issues to be noted. If you do not have much time to read an article, you should get the main point of it by reading the introduction and conclusion; this can often be more productive than attempting to skim read the whole chapter very fast.

> **TIP**
> If, from reading the introduction, you think the article is going to be useful, but want to continue your research rather than reading it there and then, you may find it useful to make bullet-pointed notes to remind yourself of exactly what it is about, to save yourself reading the same thing later.

Subheadings

Many chapters and articles contain subheadings which are useful to look through before reading the entire piece; again, this is a quick way to see where the writing is heading and think about whether all the sections will be useful.

Paragraphs

Whilst I am sure you have noted that all writing is divided into paragraphs, you may not have considered the extent to which you can use this to your advantage. Paragraphs work as miniature subsections, and should each deal with one major point. If well-constructed (as described in more detail in Chapter 5, pp. 95–7), they should consist of a statement at the beginning which introduces the main point they are going to discuss, followed by an elaboration of this point, and then a summing up before moving on to the next one. This means that it can be possible to glean the main point of a piece of writing by reading the first sentences of each paragraph; again this can often be a more successful way to 'skim read' an article, than simply flicking your eyes down the page in a less focused way.

> **Remember**   All of these skim reading strategies can be used to remind yourself of the main points a text is making.

Reading to comprehend and assess: the difficulty of reading dense texts

Targeted reading

Much of your degree will involve reading, and then formulating your own opinions about a subject in relation to the reading. First of all, however, you have to allow yourself to develop a complex understanding of the reading, which can often be difficult given the dense nature of a lot of the texts you will be asked to engage with. This section outlines ideas for ways to improve your understanding, including thoughts about effective note-making and further thinking about the notion of doing something with the text.

First of all I would suggest that the strategies for skim reading listed above can help you get a measure of the text you are reading. Rather than approaching a text one sentence at a time, with little idea of what will follow – a method that can become frustrating, time-consuming and alienating – give yourself a chance to anticipate what is coming next. This can be done by:

- Using the skim reading strategies listed above.
- Considering what part of the module your reading is related to, and making a list before you start reading it of the questions you wish to ask of the text, and the points you expect it to be dealing with.
- Finding introductory texts to outline what the particular text you are trying to read is saying. If you are reading an essay within a collection of essays, the introduction to the collection can often be helpful. Also, a lot of these books have individual introductions to the essays themselves; in this case *read the introduction*. This may sound obvious, but many people skip these introductions to 'save time', whereas often the introductions themselves can aid comprehension and thus save time in themselves.

***Doing** something with the text to keep track of the meaning*

Secondly, I would suggest making sure that none of your reading time and comprehension is wasted through a lack of good note-making, and a lack of focus. To this end, you need to develop a note-making strategy which works for you, preferably giving you a methodical approach to work your way through a text. This strategy should also help you concentrate and make sure you are understanding and taking in what you are reading, rather than reading the words on the page mechanically whilst not really registering what they are saying. There are many strategies you can experiment with and adopt. Some suggestions are given below.

● *Work from a photocopy*

Photocopy the chapter/article and highlight the sections which appear most useful and relevant. This can help you concentrate, and remember the sections you found important which you want to return to later. However, there is a danger you will just start to highlight everything when you get tired, or don't really understand what you are reading. This will render the activity useless, as you will no longer be concentrating on following the meaning, and will end up with so much highlighted text that nothing will be emphasised.

● *Annotate margins*

A companion strategy to highlighting can involve writing notes in the margins of your photocopied text to indicate why you have highlighted that particular section. These can be very brief, but if you make yourself write some kind of note *every* time you highlight, when you return to the article you will be able to remember, quickly and easily, why you highlighted in the first place.

● *Sum up each paragraph in note form*

Number each paragraph and then on a separate piece of paper next to each number write a one-sentence summary of what each one is basically saying. In this summary, you could also note down key words and critics, and whether that idea is one which connects to others useful for an assignment. It is best to try and keep these notes short, so you don't spend time copying the whole paragraph, but rather use it to make sure you understand what the writer is saying. However, if there is something in the paragraph you think you will want to quote in an essay it could be useful to write it here. This means it is of the utmost importance when using this strategy to note the author, title of book/article, publishing details and page number to ensure you can reference any material you use from the text in an assessed piece of work adequately, as well as to make sure you can find it again if you need to.

● *Track the argument using index cards*

Another way of tracking the argument whilst you are reading, and noting down salient points, is to use post-it notes or index cards. The former can be stuck on a library book, or your own without harming the paper, and can then be transferred elsewhere to help you think about the structure of the writing and your own ideas. The latter can be easily filed away for future reference, and used for revision purposes.

● *Read aloud for comprehension*

If you are really having trouble understanding a text, try reading it aloud. Although you may feel self-conscious doing this, it can be a way to approach the ideas in a different way and wake yourself and your mind up. You could also record yourself doing this, to listen back to; sometimes it helps to hear the ideas and articulate them yourself. If you have a scanner and a programme which can read text out – such as Texthelp® – you could scan in particular passages and get the computer to read them back.

● *Find a reading partner*

Try reading with someone else, discussing the text every few paragraphs to establish whether you are both in agreement with what it is saying. Discussing ideas with someone else who is also learning can really help clarify issues, as well as being an incentive for you to concentrate and helping you follow and remember what you are reading.

● *Split the text up into chunks*

If you are having real trouble with a text, don't waste time trying to read more than a few paragraphs at a time: split it up into bite-sized chunks. If it is split into relatively short subsections, try to read a subsection in one sitting, and then have a break – doing something completely different for about 10 minutes. You may have to create your own subsections or mini-deadlines to keep going – it is worth doing this rather than finding you have been staring at the text or sleeping for the last hour!

● *Look up words you don't understand*

You may find at the beginning of your degree that you are unfamiliar with a lot of the vocabulary. It can be tempting to simply skip the words you do not understand, especially if you feel pressured for time, being aware of all the other work you have to do. However, it can be counterproductive to leave these words unknown – you will learn more quickly and get to grips with your subject more efficiently if you begin to look up words you are unsure about and note down their meanings to build up a glossary for future reference. The action of looking them up and noting down the meaning should aid your memory, making it more likely that you will not only remember it the next time you see it but also that you will begin to use it. There are some subject-specific words you may come across that may not be in the ordinary dictionary, or if they are may have a more specialised meaning in the reading you are doing. It is good to acquire, or make sure you have regular access to, a subject-specific dictionary, or to note down these words to ask a tutor.

● *Keep track of the argument visually*

If you think visually, you may find it helpful to track the argument you are reading using a mindmap, or spider diagram – this can give you a visual record of the argument.

> Whichever strategy you use, make sure that your notes are good enough to remind you of the writing's salient points, before you move on to read something else.

Responding to the text

In addition to reading for comprehension, you will be reading to formulate your own opinion on a subject, meaning you need to learn to read critically. Reading critically involves allowing the texts to change the way you think, as well as interrogating what they are saying and why they saying it. It also involves making connections between texts and thinking carefully about *how* they are making an argument, and what argument they are making. This kind of critical, interrogative reading will help you keep up with lectures and contribute in seminars; it will form the largest part of preparation for your assessed work.

How can you improve your critical reading skills?

● *Ask questions of the text*

As with skim reading, and comprehension reading, to read critically it is useful to begin with a list of questions you want to ask of the text. It is useful to establish whether you expect the text to relate to others, to consider what you know of it already, and to think about what theoretical frameworks you would expect it to subscribe to.

● *Think about how the different texts relate to one another*

An effective device for structuring an argument for an essay, and for positioning your own views on a subject, is to think about the ways in which the texts you are reading connect. You may find key concepts from other texts on the module being treated in a different way in one of the texts; you may find that an idea developed by one theorist is built upon by another – or critiqued. It is useful to make a note of these moments – they can help you build your own picture about a topic as well as giving you an idea about where you fit into the critical debate.

● *Consider the way the argument is structured*

It is useful, when approaching a text critically, to consider how it is structured. Theorists, critics and philosophers all have their own ways of constructing an argument – considering why they choose a particular strategy can help you develop a more sophisticated sense of how they think, and what kinds of thinking they value, as well as helping you remember what they have said.

Consider how the argument is structured – does the writer draw upon other critics specifically? Are they concerned with developing their own theoretical concepts? If so, why? Do they use convincing examples to make their points? **No writer writes in isolation: to what other works are they referring?**

EXERCISE

Consider the following examples. What do you notice about the writing style? What does this say about the writer's agenda? Compare your thoughts to ours at the back of the book.

Example 1

The executive of the modern State is but a committee for managing the common affairs of the whole bourgeoisie.

The bourgeoisie, historically, has played a most revolutionary part.

The bourgeoisie, wherever it has got the upper hand, has put an end to all feudal, patriarchal idyllic relations. It has pitilessly torn asunder the motley feudal ties that bound man to his "natural superiors," and has left remaining no other nexus between man and man than naked self-interest, than callous "cash payment." It has drowned the most heavenly ecstasies of religious fervour, of chivalrous enthusiasm, of philistine sentimentalism, in the icy water of egotistical calculation. It has resolved personal worth into exchange value, and in place of the numberless indefeasible chartered freedoms, has set up that single, unconscionable freedom – Free Trade. In one word, for exploitation, veiled by religious and political illusions, it has substituted naked, shameless, direct, brutal exploitation.

From the *Manifesto of the Communist Party* (1848).

Exercise continued

Example 2

As much as putting out the garbage may feel like one of the most ordinary and tedious aspects of everyday life, it is a cultural perform-ance, an organized sequence of material practices, that deploys cer-tain technologies, bodily techniques and assumptions. And in this performance, waste matter is both defined and removed; a sense of order is established and a particular subject is made. Waste, then, isn't a fixed category of things; it is an effect of classification and relations.

There's nothing new in this claim: Mary Douglas made it years ago in her celebrated book *Purity and Danger*. For any study of waste this book is of singular importance. It shows how the structuring capaci-ties of culture come to classify things as waste. Douglas denatural-ized dirt and waste and places them firmly within the terrain of cultural rituals and their symbolic meanings. She shows how the values of purity and danger become lodged in specific material forms and that dirt is not outside of order but what makes systems of order visible. Who could forget her most quotable quote, "Where there is dirt there is system"?

But there is only so far you can get decoding a culture by going through the garbage. At some point the gritty materiality of waste gets under your fingernails, and the limit of classification and social construction is felt. The mountains of cheap and broken consuma-bles signify an economy utterly dependent on disposability. The greasy fast food packaging reveals the decline of home cooking. Waste becomes a social text which discloses the logic or illogic of a culture.

Gay Hawkins, *The Ethics of Waste: How we Relate to Rubbish* (Lan-ham, MD, and Oxford: Rowman & Littlefield, 2005), pp. 1–2.
Reference: Mary Douglas, *Purity and Danger* (London: Routledge & Kegan Paul, 1966)

Example 3

'So please do what I'm asking: if you state your view, you'll be doing me a favour, and also generously teaching Glaucon here and all the others too.'

My words prompted Glaucon and the others to urge him to do what I was asking, and although it was clear that Thrasymachus wanted to be heard (since he thought he had an impressive position to state, which would win him acclaim), yet he continued to dissemble and to argue that it should be me who stated my position. Eventually, however, he gave in, and then added, 'Now you can see what Socrates is good at – he refuses to do any teaching himself, but he goes around learning from other people and doesn't even give them thanks in return.'

'You're quite right to say that I learn from other people, Thrasymachus,' I said, 'but quite wrong to say that I don't repay them with gratitude. I pay them what I can – and compliments are all I can give, since I don't have money. If I think someone has a good idea, I'm quick to applaud it – as you'll find out very soon when you tell us your opinion, since I'm sure it will be a good one.'

'All right, then, listen to this,' he said. 'My claim is that morality is nothing other than the advantage of the stronger party ... Well, why aren't you applauding? No, you won't let yourself do that.'

'First I need to understand your meaning,' I told him. 'I don't yet. You say that right is the advantage of the stronger party, but what on earth do you mean by this, Thrasymachus? Surely you are not claiming, in effect, that if Poulydamas the pancratiast is stronger than us and it's to his advantage, for the sake of his physique, to eat beef, then this food is advantageous, and therefore right, for us too, who are weaker than him?'

'Foul tactics, Socrates,' he said, 'to interpret what I say in the way which allows you unscrupulously to distort it most.'

'No, you've got me wrong, Thrasymachus,' I said. 'I just want you to explain yourself better.'

Plato, *Republic*, trans. by Robin Waterfield (Oxford: Oxford University Press, 2008), pp. 19–20.

● *Be aware of the writer's agenda*

As you can see in the extract provided, Marx has a specific agenda to change society. His writing is overtly persuasive and polemical. Being aware of his agenda can help you consider the reasons for the imperatives in his writing, as well as enabling you to assess whether his argument itself is convincing. With theorists and philosophers you will rarely be the target audience, and this fact, too, should inform your reading strategy.

● *Test out ideas in the texts by applying them to your own examples*

Theoretical texts can be difficult to follow; some may seem dry and abstract unless you try and do something with the ideas with which you are being presented. Philosophers and theorists tend to use examples to demonstrate their points – these are moments which allow you to really think through the logic and implications of what they are saying. It can be useful for you to continue applying and testing out their theories with examples of your own. This can give you another way of learning the theory itself and also to consider its disadvantages and advantages.

Consider the following passage. Here the writer is thinking through the logic of what he has read, by applying it to an example.

> Structuralism ... is concerned with structures, and more particularly with examining the general laws by which they work. It ... contains a distinctive doctrine ...: the belief that the individual units of any system have meaning only by virtue of their relations to one another. This does not follow from a simple belief that you should look at things 'structurally'. You can examine a poem as a 'structure' while still treating each of its terms as more or less meaningful in itself. Perhaps the poem contains one image about the sun and another about the moon, and you are interested in how these two images fit together to form a structure. But you become a ... structuralist only when you claim that the meaning of each image is wholly a matter of its relation to the other. The images do not have a 'substantial' meaning, only a 'relational' one.
>
> Let me try to illustrate by a simple example. Suppose we are analysing a story in which a boy leaves home after quarrelling with his father, sets out on a walk through the forest in the heat of the day and falls down a deep pit. The father comes out in search of his son, peers down the pit, but is unable to see him because of the darkness. At that moment the sun has risen to a point directly overhead, illuminates the pit's depths with its rays and allows the father to rescue the child. After a joyous reconciliation, they return home together.

> ... What a structuralist critic would do [when analysing this story] would be to schematize [it] in diagrammatic form. The first unit of sig- nification, 'boy quarrels with father', might be rewritten as 'low rebels against high'. The boy's walk through the forest is a movement along a horizontal axis, in contrast to the vertical axis 'low/high', and could be indexed as 'middle'. The fall into the pit, a place below ground, signifies 'low' again, and the zenith of the sun 'high'. By shining into the pit, the sun has in a sense stooped 'low', thus inverting the narrative's first signi- fying unit, where 'low' struck against 'high'. The reconciliation between father and son restores equilibrium between 'low' and 'high', and the walk home together, signifying 'middle', marks this achievement of a suitably intermediate state.

Terry Eagleton, *Literary Theory: An Introduction* (Oxford: Blackwell, 1983), pp. 94–5.

Eagleton uses his own example to illustrate the way structuralism works – this is an example you could write out as a diagram in your notes, to learn about the theory. However, it is also a way you could think about Eagleton's *take* on the theory – do you agree that 'structuralism' is this simplistic? This is the kind of passage you could critique in your own analysis of the theory – perhaps coming up with your own examples or analyses to respond to Terry Eagleton's and so show you are a critical reader.

● Reading creative and visual texts – how to develop your own interpretation

As this chapter has emphasised, reading involves both understanding and interpreting. In other words, as well as trying to understand what a text is saying, you need to develop your own opinion about how it is saying it, and what you think about the message it is conveying. We have focused mostly on theoretical and critical texts, but for many Arts subjects your central focus will be creative products – be they fiction, poetry, paintings, photographs, sculpture, films (and the list goes on). You will need to learn how to develop your own response to these, using the secondary material recommended by tutors, but also by reading these creative and visual texts yourself. In my experience, the students most confident about expressing their opinion in seminars and in writing are the ones who have given time to really thinking about their own response to a creative text, before going to read what others have said about it.

How can you develop your own opinion?

- Give yourself time to read and re-read the text, before going to read what others have said. Make notes about your initial response, and write down any questions it might have raised.

- Think about the way it is presented – if a written text, is there anything notable about the writing style? If a painting or photograph, what is interesting about the colours used, the light, the shapes, the perspective, the use of space? If a film or play, you could think, again about colour and light, as well as costume, perspective, the kind of shots used, the music and sound effects. What is the effect of all of these?

- Consider the structure – how is the story told? How is the visual text constructed? Are there particular images or symbols which are used repeatedly?

- Is there anything surprising or unusual worth noting?

- Compare the text to others? Does it contrast significantly with others you have considered from the same genre or period? Is it particularly similar to others? In what ways? Is it typical of the author/artist's work, or significantly different?

- What issues is it dealing with?

- Think about the different messages it could be conveying – what does it mean? For example, does it have a particular moral message? Is it saying something about the function of art? Is it commenting on a particular political situation? Or a theory? Is it saying something about human relationships?

- What questions does it raise?

You may not be able to deal with all of these issues straight away – and particularly at the beginning of your degree it can be difficult to form opinions. You may find creative texts raise more questions than you have answers for. Don't worry, you are at university to learn. Make a note of your initial questions and use these to guide your secondary and theoretical readings. Raise these in seminars. But don't abandon the questions – use them to investigate. The way you investigate will be unique to you: this will be the beginning of your contribution to the subject. Embrace these moments of research and discovery and keep track of your thought process. You have interesting things to say: if you allow time to develop your own opinion through reading you will find ways to say them.

● Summary

In this chapter, I have highlighted the need to read often, to read carefully and to read critically. Also, I have suggested ways to keep track of your reading, and to develop your own opinion. This can be done by *re*reading, in Roland Barthes' sense – by reading each text as unique, thinking about how it is written as well as what it is saying. I will leave you with Barthes' thoughts on reading.

> Rereading, an operation contrary to the commercial and ideological habits of our society, which would have us throw away the story once it has been consumed (devoured) so that we can then move onto another story, buy another book, and which is tolerated only in certain marginal categories of readers (children, old people, and professors), rereading is here suggested at the outset, for it alone saves the text from repetition (those who fail to reread are obliged to see the same story everywhere).
>
> Roland Barthes, *S/Z*, trans. by Richard Miller (New York: Hill & Wang, 1974), pp. 15–16.

Try and made sure you *re*read, rather than consume, discard and forget.

4 Written Assignments 1: What is Expected of You?

● Introduction

Even before you arrived at university, you will no doubt have suspected that written assignments would form a large part of your degree. You may discover when you arrive, perhaps with a degree of shock, that you are asked to tackle an essay or a report very early on in your course – possibly in the first few weeks. What is your reaction going to be to such an assignment? Maybe you are ready to get your teeth into a new challenge. Maybe (and I suspect this is true for many new students) you are a little worried at the prospect of writing your first essay. Maybe you feel that you are the only person who doesn't know what they are supposed to be doing. These are entirely natural reactions to have. Most people, when facing a new challenge, experience some degree of nervousness; venturing into the unknown can be a scary move.

The first thing to say is, "Don't panic!" Your tutors and lecturers know that you are in the early stages of your degree and are not yet expert in the discipline or in the way in which an academic essay should be written. Early assignments in your first term are given, not just to 'test' you on what you have read, researched, and understood in the course of your lectures and study time, but to give you an opportunity to practise having a go at writing essays. So you should try to approach your early assignments in the spirit of 'Well, even if I'm not sure exactly what I should be doing, I'm going to give it a go and see what happens.'

Have *you* had any of these thoughts?
"What if I'm not good enough?!"
"Everybody else knows what they are doing – I'm the only one who doesn't!"
"I don't know what my lecturers are looking for in an essay/assignment!"

Most people have thoughts like these! You're not alone and you should try not to worry too much. If you are really concerned, you should try to find a friendly person in your department that you can talk to – your personal tutor, a lecturer or tutor or a senior student.

And what, indeed, is the worst that can happen? You are not going to fail your degree by writing one slightly dodgy essay. In fact, it is doubtful that you could even fail a module on the basis of one essay (though I would urge you to verify this fact before you start). No one is going to laugh at you or think you are incapable. You *are* capable! You have been selected to study at your university on the basis of your academic credentials. Those credentials will be largely the same or comparable to your peers, your fellow students. All first years are in the same boat.

Many university courses do not 'count' the first year in the final degree classification – this means the marks that you receive in your first year will not have an impact on your final degree mark. You can see why this is a sensible policy for universities to adopt; it gives the most junior students the opportunity to 'have a go' at assignments with minimal risk. You do not arrive at university in Freshers' Week with the level of skills that you need to pass a degree – you develop the skills throughout your time at university. Do not feel as though you are alone in being 'thrown in the deep end' (if that is indeed how you feel). You will acquire the skills and the knowledge you need to pass your degree by using the resources that are available to you: through some reading, some hard work, some independent study, and through listening to the feedback of your tutors. You *will* get there and when you graduate you will be able to look back on your development and feel that, although the learning curve was maybe a steep one, you were able to overcome the challenges that you faced.

● Alternatives to essays

Essays are the dominant form of assessment for Arts and Humanities subjects, and the majority of this chapter will be addressing these explicitly. However, you may be required, throughout your degree, to write assignments in a form different from conventional essays. The three most common alternatives – apart from dissertations, which we will address later – are *reports*, *review articles* and *gobbets* (or small pieces of writing, usually consisting of one-paragraph responses). For each of these alternatives, as for essays, you should follow the guidelines given to you by your tutors as much as you can – checking with them any details or issues to do with the format that you do not understand (including how they will be marked). However, whilst much of the advice on essays we will give in these two chapters would be useful for all written assessments, we present brief guidelines here about what is generally expected of these main alternatives.

Reports

A report involves making an assessment of a situation, and then providing recommendations. Whereas in an essay you will be developing a discursive argument in continuous prose, a report usually has different subheaded sections in which the situation being reported on is outlined, and critically analysed, before an investigation takes place and recommendations are made.

An important question to consider when writing a report is, "Who is your imagined or intended audience?" In the professional world reports are often commissioned by a government body, a company, or an organisation to be used as a basis for changes to be made, and matters to be investigated. So, if you imagine who your audience is, and why they might need the report, then you can think about what you need to write in order to provide an appropriate investigative structure. In summary, a report differs from an essay in that it is designed to provide information which will be acted on, rather than to be read by people interested in the ideas for their own sake. Because of this, it has a different structure and layout.

It is impossible for me to outline a foolproof structure for you to follow when writing a report, as it really depends upon what your department requires. However, reports usually contain:

An **abstract** – a single paragraph outlining the main subject the report is addressing, the way it is addressing it, and the conclusions it reaches.

An **introduction**, **literature review**, **methodology section** – this outlines the issues to be addressed and the main reasons for addressing them. It often includes a theoretical overview – in other words it can be there to give context for the research described in the main report, giving reasons for the method of research chosen, and considering related reports to sum up what has been found out about the subject so far.

An **analysis** and **presentation of findings** – this presents any findings from the research, and analyses of these findings. Sometimes these processes are separated into 'Results' and 'Discussion'. What I can say here is that you will need to find a way to sum up what you have found, and then analyse what is important or significant or relevant about these findings.

Conclusions, **recommendations** – this final section will involve summing up the most important findings, and thinking about what overall conclusions can be drawn. This should involve referring back to ideas brought up in the introduction and literature review. Reports usually end with a set of recommendations – how has your research caused you to view the situation differently? Could things be changed or viewed differently? What further research needs to be done?

Reviews and review articles

A good review involves a critical assessment of a cultural product or situation. To do this you need to provide context, and make clear how you will be assessing. Think about the reviews you have come across in newspapers for books, restaurants, exhibitions. These all have some implied criteria, such as – if we take books as an example – Is the book clearly written? Is it interesting? Does it achieve what it sets out to do? Reviews also put their subject matter into context – How does it compare to other, similar books? Does it provide something new? Is it ahead in its field or is it simply repeating what others have said? Does it have something unique to say? Review articles play a similar role, but usually require you to provide even more context. You may be asked to review a situation, through reviewing the literature on the subject, or you may be asked to review a specific article. The structure of an article will most likely be the same as an essay, but a shorter review often has to be more succinct.

Common structure for a shorter review

- Succinctly introduce the general area for discussion.
- Begin by describing the thing that you are reviewing; make clear through your language what you think of it.
- Make direct statements of assessment about the thing you are reviewing.
- Sum up with your conclusions – these do not have to be excessive praise or critique. They could involve a balanced assessment such as 'whilst the book is disappointing in these ways ... it would be useful to anyone looking for information about this.'

Common structure for a review article

Introduction – indicate the structure of the discussion about to take place, and make clear what will be argued.

Discussion – sum up the literature on the subject. If reviewing an historical critique, for example, this could involve clarifying the different perspectives and analysing the one which seems the most useful.

Conclusion – provide a final analysis clarifying your position. This could also involve putting forward recommendations for further reading, research to be undertaken, or better ways to view the subject at hand.

The most important thing to remember with any review is that it is your opportunity to provide your own assessment of a situation – so you need to put time into deciding what you think, and then consider carefully the most effective way to present this. Many sections of this chapter will help you become better at articulating your own opinion, in particular, take a look at **Developing your critical voice** (p. 82).

Gobbets

You might be given a written assignment or a 'gobbet' if you are taking a course in History or its allied disciplines. These usually require short analyses (500 words or so) of primary source material: whether texts or pictures. Your tutor will provide you with guidance about what they are looking for in your analysis, but in general, you would need to demonstrate knowledge of the meaning and purpose of the source material; a solid understanding of its context and, most importantly, a critical analysis crisply conveyed.

● What makes a good essay?

In the second part of this chapter, I offer some advice on how to begin the process of writing your essay, but before that it might be useful to point out some major features that any good essay will exhibit. Having a think about these features before you begin, and reminding yourself of them as you go along, will provide you with some sort of framework to work within. So what makes a good essay? Well, an essay is a written composition, a piece of writing on a specific topic. It will nearly always involve constructing an *argument*. This is perhaps *the most* important thing to remember when planning your essay. A question is posed (the essay title), a response is made, supporting evidence is offered, and a conclusion is then reached. There will not be *one right answer* to the question asked by the title of your essay, but the quality of your essay will depend on how successfully you argue for your conclusion (i.e. the answer that you think is the right one). This means that, although there may be no one right answer, it *doesn't* mean that 'anything goes'. It *doesn't* mean that you can write *absolutely anything* in response to the question and still be right, and be awarded a good mark.

Arts and Humanities subjects require you to demonstrate your *critical abilities* – indeed, criticism is the *hallmark* of these disciplines (and this is what you will find in your lecturers' books and journal articles). The way that you can demonstrate your critical abilities is through the quality of your argumentation; do you provide a convincing, coherent and comprehensive argument?

Table 4.1 lists some features of a good essay. When you've had a go at your first piece of work see how far your essay exhibits these features and use it as a checklist. Don't be put off just yet, though; the rest of this chapter will help you with each of these features. Page references for the relevant section of the chapter are given in Table 4.1. If you are struggling with a particular feature, skip on ahead to read some advice.

● What are different essay questions asking for?

The first thing the checklist asks you to do is *respond to the question* asked by the title of the essay. This might sound *completely* obvious, but you would be surprised how many people fail to do this very simple thing! Many, many students fall at this first hurdle, and here is why: they don't read the title carefully. These students tend to pick out a key word – say it is an essay about Shakespeare's *Henry V*. They then proceed to write *everything they know* about *Henry V*, or everything that they can remember having been said in lectures, in no particular order, hoping that their tutor will be able to pick something worthwhile out of the mass of information that is presented. These students hope that just because they are writing about the *topic* they will somehow deserve to be given credit for their answer. Unfortunately, they are absolutely wrong and this strategy is a dangerous one – even if what they have written is factually correct! If your tutor wanted you to recount everything you know about a particular topic, then they wouldn't have gone to the bother of coming up with an essay question.

And this brings us back to the most important point about writing essays. That is, that your essay, whatever its topic, must contain more than mere *information*. **It must contain an argument.** This goes for *all* discursive essays in the Arts and Humanities: whether you are answering a question about *Henry V*, Modernist poetry, the Napoleonic Wars, Aristotelian ethics, French *New Wave* Film, or whatever.

So it is essential to understand what you are being asked to do before embarking on the preparation for a written assignment. Your first task is to read the assignment instructions as carefully as possible and ask your tutor about anything you find confusing: this can be done in a seminar situation or within the tutor's consultation hours. There are many different kinds of essay titles, but most of them use a common vocabulary, what might be called *key words*. These will crop up time and again (in exams too), so you need to be able to understand what these key words mean.

Content	Page numbers	Checklist
Responds to the question asked by the title	70, 72	
Responds to the question asked by the title by proposing *an argument*	70, 94	
Provides support for the argument in the form of *evidence* (e.g. from texts, or primary sources) or provides support for the argument in the form of *reasons*	109–111	
Provides support for the argument in the form of *relevant* evidence and reasons	109–111	
Uses a sufficient range of sources	94	
Demonstrates your own independent thinking and analysis: your own 'critical voice'	82–89	
Correctly references any sources, both in a list of references and in the bibliography	111–115	
Structure		
Is structured in such a way that it has an introduction, middle and conclusion	98–109	
Has an introduction that accurately indicates the structure and direction of the essay's main argument	98–99	
Builds upon the argument, paragraph by paragraph	96–96	
Style		
Has a flowing style; one paragraph leads logically onto the next and does not jar when you read the essay out loud	95–96, 115	
Is clearly written; there are no rambling sentences, repetition, waffle or words that you don't know the meaning of	78–82, 126, 134	
Is fully spell-checked	115	
Has everything on the title page which is needed (your name, name of tutor and module, word count, assignment title etc.)	115	

Table 4.1   Some features of a good essay

Figure 4.1 displays a glossary of some of the main instructional words you are likely to encounter and the key meanings of those terms.

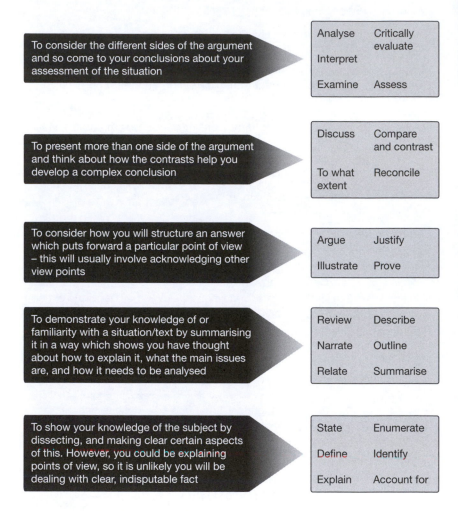

To consider the different sides of the argument and so come to your conclusions about your assessment of the situation	Analyse	Critically evaluate
	Interpret	
	Examine	Assess

| To present more than one side of the argument and think about how the contrasts help you develop a complex conclusion | Discuss | Compare and contrast |
| | To what extent | Reconcile |

| To consider how you will structure an answer which puts forward a particular point of view – this will usually involve acknowledging other view points | Argue | Justify |
| | Illustrate | Prove |

To demonstrate your knowledge of or familiarity with a situation/text by summarising it in a way which shows you have thought about how to explain it, what the main issues are, and how it needs to be analysed	Review	Describe
	Narrate	Outline
	Relate	Summarise

To show your knowledge of the subject by dissecting, and making clear certain aspects of this. However, you could be explaining points of view, so it is unlikely you will be dealing with clear, indisputable fact	State	Enumerate
	Define	Identify
	Explain	Account for

Figure 4.1   Key instructional words and their meanings

● Defining your terms

In all likelihood, your essay title or topic will contain words that need *defining*. It is very important to define key terms so that:

- You show you understand them.
- You let your reader know *how* you are using them.
- You alert your reader to terms that may be problematic, ambiguous, or subject to change over time (or within particular contexts).

A good place to define key terms in an essay is in the introduction or the opening paragraphs in the main body. Consider these two examples.

Extract 1

The Chinese approach is initially more social. Humanity is social. A social *dao* ('way') guides us. Chinese ethical thinkers reflect on how to preserve, transmit or change this way – the public, guiding discourse. When modern Chinese writers sought a translation for 'ethics', they chose the compound term *dao de* – ways and virtues. *Dao* is public, objective guidance. *De* ('virtue') consists of the character traits, skills, and dispositions induced by exposure to a *dao*. *De* is the physical realization of *dao* in some part of the human system – a family, a state, or an individual. We may get virtue either by internalizing a way or it may be inborn.

Both *dao* and *de* encompass more than morality proper. There are ways of fashion, etiquette, archery, economics, and prudence. Both *dao* and *de* can have negative connotations, e.g. when speaking of the ways of one's opponents. Most Chinese writers, however, use *dao* in speaking of their own system for guiding behaviour and most take the social point of view. Translations, as a rule, therefore, treat *dao* as a definite description. They write '*The Way*' when they find *dao* in a text. (Classical Chinese has no definite article.) This causes difficulty if we remember that the different schools disagreed about *which* way was *the* way.

From the introductory paragraphs of 'Classical Chinese Ethics' by Chad Hansen in Peter Singer (ed.), *A Companion to Ethics* (London: Blackwell, 1993), p. 69.

The writer, in this instance, has explained the complex meanings and the relationship of *dao* and *de* and in doing so has indicated what the essay will be about (in part the difficulty of the different schools disagreeing about which way was *the* way). The writer demonstrates that understanding the different ways in which *dao* and *de* are defined by the different schools is crucial to a critical approach to the subject.

> **Extract 2**
>
> Bodies rarely figure in autobiography. Even movie stars – those icons of an ideal body and of the material, emotional, and sexual sustenance it can earn its keeper – tend in their autobiographies to minimize the significance of their bodies to their personal and professional lives … The histories of autobiography and of its criticism tend to construe the self as individuated and coherent rather than as the product of social construction and as a subject-in-process and work consistently toward repression of the representation of bodies in autobiography.
>
> From '"An appearance walking in a forest the sexes burn": Autobiography and the Construction of the Feminine Body' by Shirley Neuman in Kathleen Ashley, Leigh Gilmore and Gerald Petters (eds), *Autobiography and Postmodernism* (Boston: University of Massachusetts Press, 1994), p. 293.

The writer in this example first qualifies what she means by her reference to movie stars, by using the dashes to allow for further explanation (thus allowing the reader to follow her train of thought). She then goes on to discuss how the 'histories of autobiography' have conceived of and represented the self. In this way she begins to show the complexity of defining 'autobiography' and the 'self' (each definition will rely on the other and both are subject to specific social and historical context).

Where can you find reliable definitions of words?

When writing you should get into the habit of using good reference sources to make sure you acknowledge the complexity of the terms you are using, and write in a precise way. The *Oxford English Dictionary*, which should be available in your university library both in hard copy and online, is a good place to start when beginning to define a term. It provides the etymology (the historical origins of the word) as well as quotations with date charts which indicate the history of its usage.

However, whilst the *Oxford English Dictionary* outlines the most common usages of a term, it may not be so useful for words which have been adopted by key theorists, or different academic disciplines, to signify meanings specific to particular contexts. This is why it is always useful to get in the habit of consulting reference texts specific to your subject, as well as concentrating upon the way your tutors discuss the ambiguity of particular terms.

Take care! Defining words can be tricky

Some words have a whole variety of meanings, some very particular to one discipline

In English literature the word 'romantic' can be used in a number of ways, signifying a number of different, specific meanings when referring to kinds of literary writing, as well as methods of reading. The *Concise Oxford Dictionary* (9th edition) lists the following definitions:

> of, characterized by, or suggestive of an idealized, sentimental, or fantastic view of reality; remote from experience (*a romantic picture; a romantic setting*). **2** inclined towards or suggestive of romance in love (*a romantic woman; a romantic evening; romantic words*). **3** (of a person) imaginative, visionary, idealistic. **4 a.** (of style, in art, music, etc.) concerned more with feeling and emotion than with form and aesthetic qualities; preferring grandeur and picturequeness to finish and proportion. **b.** (also **Romantic**) of or relating to the 18th–19th-c. romantic movement of style in the European arts. **5** (of a project etc.) unpractical, fantastic. n. **1** a romantic person. **2** a romanticist. **romantically** adv. [*romant* 'tale of chivalry' from Old French, from *romanz* romance]

The dictionary identifies the everyday meanings of romantic, as well as the literary connotations, but does not elaborate on what the 18th–19th-century style of writing involved. So, if considering literature you would need to turn to a reference source designed for literature in particular. There are numerous sources for literature. For example, the one I used as a student – *The Penguin Dictionary of Literary Terms and Literary Theory* – dedicates about four pages to 'romanticism'; this indicates how difficult it is to define. These dictionary definitions also emphasise the way a word's meaning can change over time. As the editor J.A. Cuddon puts it:

> The American scholar A.O. Lovejoy once observed that the word 'romantic' has come to mean so many things that, by itself, it means nothing at all ... The variety of its actual and possible meanings and connotations reflects the complexity and multiplicity of European romanticism.
>
> *The Penguin Dictionary of Literary Terms and Literary Theory*
> (London: Penguin, 1992) p. 813.

My point here, then, is that when using a term like this, you need to make yourself aware of the complexity of the term, the ways it has been used, and make it clear in your own writing how you are using it.

Some theorists choose to use a word which is commonly understood to mean one thing, to mean something very particular to their own theory

For example, the linguistic scholar, Julia Kristeva, in her theories about the relationship between the body and poetic language, appropriates the word 'semiotic'. A dictionary definition of semiotic would have it to be an adjective referring to 'semiotics: the study of signs and symbols in various fields, coming from the Greek "of signs"'. However, Kristeva makes it more complicated – whilst she 'understands the term "semiotic" in its Greek sense' – she provides her *own* interpretation within this list of connecting words: 'distinctive mark, trace, index, precursory sign, proof, engraved or written sign, imprint, trace, figuration' ('Revolution in Poetic Language', *The Kristeva Reader*, ed. Toril Moi, trans. Seàn Hand (London: Blackwell, 1986) p. 96). She then connects this idea of the 'sign' to the body, arguing that these signs make messages through the body which ultimately become the 'symbolic', when they are read by others. If you were writing about Kristeva's notion of the semiotic, again, it would not be sufficient to consult the dictionary for a definition, it would be necessary to consider Kristeva's own definition and, if you find this unclear, research how other people have interpreted her use of this word.

You may come across a word which is not in the dictionary, because the person using it has made up their own term

You may come across one of a number of influential thinkers who make up their own terms to characterise something key to their theory. These terms usually remain ambiguous to readers of the theorists – open to interpretation – and so they are in the continual process of re-definition by the different critics who use them. For example, take this section from the English translation of Roland Barthes' book on photography, *Camera Lucida: Reflections on Photography*:

What I feel about these photographs derives from an average affect, almost from a certain training. I did not know a French word which might account for this kind of human interest, but I believe this word exists in Latin: it is *studium*, which doesn't mean, at least not immediately, "study," but application to a thing, taste for someone, a kind of general, enthusiastic commitment, of course, but without special acuity. It is by *studium* that I am interested in so many photographs, whether I receive them as political testimony or enjoy them as good historical scenes: for it is culturally (this connotation is present in *studium*) that I participate in the figures, the faces, the gestures, the settings, the actions.

The second element will break (or punctuate) the *studium*. This time it is not I who seek it out (as I invest the field of the *studium* with my sovereign consciousness), it is this element which rises from the scene, shoots out of it like an arrow, and pierces me. A Latin word exists to designate this wound, this prick, this mark made by a pointed instrument: the word suits me all the better in that it also refers to the notion of punctuation, and because the photographs I am speaking of are in effect punctuated, sometimes even speckled with these sensitive points; precisely, these marks, these wounds are so many *points*. This second element which will disturb the *studium* I shall therefore call *punctum*; for *punctum* is also: sting, speck, cut, little hole – and also a cast of the dice. A photograph's *punctum* is that accident which pricks me (but also bruises me, is poignant to me).

Camera Lucida: Reflections on Photography, trans. by Richard Howard
(London: Random House, 2000), pp. 25–7.

Not only is this a great example of Roland Barthes defining his terms, and so making his complex distinctions about his experiences of looking at a photograph, clear and understandable; it also here to give you an example of a couple of words you will not find easily in a dictionary. Barthes draws upon Latin to try and explain what he means. But he also then provides his own definitions of the words – if you were writing about Barthes' theory of photography, or referring to Barthes when writing about your own thoughts on photography, the above definitions of *studium* and *punctum* are the ones you would need to think about when providing your own interpretations in writing.

And this brings me to my final point: it is important that you define your terms because language is slippery, and it can never completely contain experience. As Benjamin Whorf put it '[N]o individual is free to describe nature with complete impartiality but is constrained to certain modes of interpretation even while he thinks himself most free' (*Language, Thought and Reality*, New York: MIT Press, 1956, p. 214). Language can never fully explain or describe the world – theorists and poets often manipulate it to deal with this situation; as a reader and writer, you necessarily become part of the community of people who think about the way language is used, and aim to use it as precisely as possible. All the way through your writing career at university you need to be careful that you say what you mean. Language and the meaning of language is always shifting. The best way to deal with this potentially disconcerting fact is to be aware of it, acknowledge it, and embrace it by spending time in your reading looking up the meanings of words you are unsure of, and in your writing ensuring you make clear how you are using your key terms.

● Writing clearly in an academic style

Writing clearly and making your points understood can be difficult. Most students, when they first get to university, struggle with developing a writing style that successfully conveys what they mean, whilst also delivering what the tutor expects. Developing your writing style is an important transferable skill that you can take from an Arts and Humanities degree. Most tutors will give you feedback on your writing style, as well as comment upon the ideas in your assignments. If you do not write clearly your tutors will not understand what you are trying to say. In order to do your ideas justice, you should spend some time thinking about and learning how to write clearly and precisely.

> Unclear writing is often the product of unclear thinking. If you are not quite sure what your argument is, or you do not quite understand a theory you are trying to outline, this is usually conveyed in confusing sentence structures, and vague, generalised remarks. Sometimes, you may only be able to clarify what you mean to yourself through writing. Ensure you give yourself enough time to edit so the work you hand in is as coherent as possible. Much imprecise writing comes from poor planning, or rushed work, so if you are keen to do your ideas justice give sufficient time to the writing process.

In an attempt to sound academic, some students turn to their thesauruses to find complex ways of saying quite straightforward things, unfortunately obscuring their meaning in the process. Some go to the other extreme, working from the maxim 'write how you speak' and end up sounding too casual, and not formal enough for an academic assessment. Both of these reactions to the challenges of written assessment are understandable, because the writing process is difficult; it can seem intimidating to show your written work to academic professionals who will then assess it. Take time to find a writing style with which you are comfortable. It is good to remember, then, that learning to write is a process and it is a process which will be helped by taking the advice you receive from tutors seriously, and paying attention to the guidelines in your handbooks. I've also got some recommendations in this section.

Below I list and discuss some bad habits it is easy to fall into when producing written work. Don't let this list become too daunting – it is designed to help you think about why your tutors will reward certain kinds of writing, and criticise others. If you write well, you communicate your ideas effectively, and your tutors can spend time responding *to* these ideas.

Bad habits to avoid

1. Redundant and repetitive phrases

Examples are:

> *I shall now show* – just show it!
> *It is rather important to realise* – this is very wordy; the 'rather' at the very least could be taken out
> *As I described above* – sometimes you might need to put 'as already mentioned' but try to suggest this in the least possible words
> *I think, perhaps, that* – this suggests an unfinished thought rather than a confident, complete argument

These phrases tend to get in the way of what you are trying to say, and take up words which could be used to push your argument on. Most of the time, they can just be cut altogether. They often have the effect of making the writer seem a bit under-confident, making the reader think 'just get on with it'! I often find myself using these phrases in my first draft and then cutting them out at the end. This is what makes the editing process so important. Many people think while they write – as discussed in **The Art of Drafting**, Chapter 5 (p. 91). This is fine, as long as you give yourself time to *edit* before handing the work in: take out words which were necessary for your own thinking process, but which are not necessary for a reader to see.

2. Colloquial language

Although writing as you speak can be a useful way to get ideas down onto paper in the first place, many phrases and certain ways of speaking which are acceptable in everyday conversation may not be appropriate in academic writing. In the examples below, the words in bold would be wholly acceptable in normal speech, but a more disciplined, formal style is required in a university written assignment:

Luckily *this form of drama* – sounds too chatty, and is a bit ambiguous; lucky for who? A more precise term could be used.

This is of **course** – 'of course' is problematic because what is obvious to the writer is not always so obvious to the reader; it is also too informal.

Hopefully *I will have shown you* – this sounds a bit too under-confident, and self-deprecating; try and be confident about the fact you have made your point.

We should not try to **squeeze** *too much meaning into one speech* – a more precise term could be used.

Alternative constructions would be:

The form of drama fortunately has the means of
This is certainly
The point in question has been demonstrated
It is important not to attempt to compress too much meaning into one speech

3. Vague statements and over-generalisations

It is easy to fall into the trap – especially when writing the first draft of an assignment – of making comments which are so obvious they do not mean anything of significance. It is also tempting, when trying to sound as though you have authority over the subject, to make large over-arching claims about a topic that you could not really support with evidence. Try to look out for these when proofreading your work. Think about whether each claim you make can and has been justified, whether it plays a useful part in the construction of your argument and whether it is made in the most precise and succinct way. For example:

Dozens of books have been written over the years about this subject by numerous authors – this statement is too vague to mean anything, and suggests the writer has not really researched their topic sufficiently. It might be more effective to say 'this subject has captured the interest of a number of critics, for example ...'. This grounds the point with specific information the reader could go and find more about, also demonstrating the writer has undertaken scholarly research.

Various examples have been seen in many parts of the country through-out the years – again, it would be better to pick out some examples and specify the years more precisely.

The Renaissance period was a time of change – this is not a useful insight; what kind of change? Also, every time period contains change, so it does not say anything precise enough to convey useful information about the Renaissance.

Since the dawn of time, man has searched for meaning – never start an essay with these words!

In summary, when you are writing in an academic style, you should assume a confident tone, showing that the facts and ideas being dealt with have been carefully researched and thought through.

Feeling ambitious?

There are a few strategies you can use to really develop your writing style, so that it becomes a means for conveying complex ideas effectively. For example, you might:

- Start to build up a bank of words which could provide academic alternatives to colloquialisms (more casual chatty language). These could be found in a thesaurus or dictionary. You might find alternatives are also suggested by tutors (if they are not but tutors have complained about a word – go and ask them what they would use as an alternative).

- Try to make every sentence *count*. Every sentence in an essay must work – it must contribute to the argument. When reading through your work, think about whether every sentence really does add something. Read published chapters and articles and think critically about how each sentence contributes to the overall passage.

- Find academic writing you *like*, and take note of particular phrasing, sentence structure, ways to introduce ideas and quotations. I also found myself writing down sentences I liked in lectures, and even noting down the way other students put things. Learning to write is a collaborative process – utilise the great resources you have at university in the library, your discussion groups and other learning situations.

- Get into the habit of noting the advice of your tutors and friends. Don't shy away from showing your work to them. All professional writers show their work to others – no writing is produced in a vacuum. Your writing will improve much more rapidly if you consistently put it through the rigour of critique from others. Just make sure this does not result in you only seeing the negative in your writing – remember what people liked about your writing too.

● Developing your critical voice

Although you will be taking modules with other people, and quite possibly be undertaking exactly the same degree programme as others, your degree experience will be unique to you. This is because, whilst Arts and Humanities modules are usually designed to introduce you to a set of core themes, ideas, theories and texts, their ultimate aim is to get you to develop your own critical voice. What do we mean by critical voice? Well, this could be understood as your own personal take on your subject and your degree as a whole.

In your degree you will need to navigate your own way through the different modules that you take, and the different ideas you will develop, with a variety of tutors and students. Each should help you think about your subject in new interesting ways, but ultimately you will be making decisions about what you think, and seeing your own connections between subjects. If you track these decisions and connections carefully, you will be able to see your own critical voice developing. Everything you learn will become context for the new subjects you approach. The more you think about one subject, the more tools you will have to interrogate another. In this way you will develop your own critical voice.

What is critical thinking?

Thinking critically involves:

- dealing with complex notions;
- making connections between ideas;
- analysing the arguments of others;
- putting your own argument within the context of a wider debate;
- being prepared to question your own assumptions and the assumptions of others;
- weighing up the pros and cons of different theories and making decisions about which ones you find most convincing and why;
- taking on board the ideas of others while developing new ones of your own;.
- discerning implicit as well as explicit meanings.

> **Critical thinking necessarily involves non-binary thinking.**

What is binary thinking?

To put it simply, binary thinking involves dividing ideas into opposites: right and wrong, black and white, good and bad – and deciding you can judge a text, a person, a movement, a set of ideas, an action on these terms only. Here are some common binaries as identified by Hélène Cixous in 'Sorties', in E. Marks and I. Courtiviron, *New French Feminisms*, trans. A. Liddle (Amherst, MA: University of Massachusetts Press, 1980), p. 90:

Activity/Passivity	Father/Mother	Nature/History
Sun/Moon	Head/Heart	Nature/Art
Culture/Nature	Man/Woman	Nature/Mind
Day/Night		

Here are a few of my own:

Right/Wrong
Good/Bad
Valuable/Rubbish

There are problems with these kinds of division, as the world is more complicated than this. You will be continually coming across situations in which it is very difficult or even impossible to make a clear-cut judgement about something.

Think about these three examples.

Example 1
A trolley has been abandoned in the street and is slightly bashed up. Is it rubbish? After all it is abandoned and does not work as well as it did? Is it property? We know it must have belonged to a supermarket at some point. And what if someone starts using it – as a transporter, or as material to turn into art – how can we then define it?

Example 2
A child adopted at birth finds out her birth mother wants to meet her. She does not feel any attachment to the mother and does not want to meet her. Her adopted mother thinks she should meet her birth mother, as she might regret the missed opportunity later. She does not think the birth mother has a right to develop a relationship with her. Should they meet? Is her birth mother never to be forgiven for giving her up as a child? Is it even a case for forgiveness? Should the child not just meet her for her own benefit? Is there a simple right or wrong answer to this question?

Example 3

Shakespeare's play *The Tempest* is set on an island with three human inhabitants: Prospero (self-appointed ruler who has learnt magic to wield control), Miranda (Prospero's daughter), Caliban (an inhabitant of the island who arrived a long time before the other two). We learn from Prospero and Miranda that the three maintained amicable relations until Caliban attempted to rape Miranda: this resulted in Prospero making him his slave. How do we read this situation? Can we rely on Prospero's version of events? Is Caliban evil? Is slavery ever justified? Could it not be said that Caliban had already become enslaved before the incident with Miranda since he had lost ownership of the island? Is one act of attempted violence enough to condemn Caliban to a life of slavery? Did Caliban commit this action to try and gain some control? Should we feel sympathy for Prospero once we find out he has been betrayed by his brother and lost his position as Duke of Milan? Critics and directors of the play have to address these questions and justify their final interpretations; there are no definitive answers.

It would not be appropriate to use binary thinking (property/rubbish, right/wrong, nature/nurture) to try and come up with the 'right' answer to any of these situations. Instead a considered judgement would need to be made by weighing up the situation, taking into account how convincing the ideas of others are, and so presenting a well thought-through discussion of the situation.

How can binary thinking be avoided?

You need to allow yourself to think in a more flexible way, allowing for uncertainties, ambiguity, questions to be asked, alternatives to be considered, other thoughts to be taken into account. This can be achieved by recognising that situations can be more complicated than they may at first seem, and by beginning to identify when you think other people could be engaging in overly simplistic binary thinking.

In your degree you will begin to do well if you start using your imaginative and analytical skills to go beyond simplistic thinking – which reduces the discussion to right/wrong binaries – and allow your own argument to account for and contain complexities. In your writing, how can you do this?

How to think and write critically

To help you consider how to incorporate critical thinking in your essay writing, in this section I have included four examples from students' work. These demonstrate some good practice, but please bear in mind, however, that they are not model answers. Try to think about the structure of each example and don't worry if you are unfamiliar with the subject.

Make your own judgements about a situation by taking into account those of others

Example essay

[1]Looking closer at the idea that co-talking can be misogynistic reveals that the roots of the problem lie not in language or gender (as Bond suggests), but once more derive from nationality and the unfortunate influence of 'twoness'. [2]DuPlessis's essay comes extraordinarily close to saying this without making the final link: that the very 'represented power' of the men's signifying talk lends itself to further potential compensation and [re] empowerments, through sexual superiority. [3]Considering Janie's trials she observes that the black men's desire to dominate women is a displacement of the power they are denied racially, the (white ruled) trial having 'done them out of their self-proclaimed substitute: their gender privilege, which can include rights of possession, and sexual arousals enforced by wife-beating…'. But despite recognising elsewhere that language is 'the only real weapon left to weak [i.e. African American] folks' (p. 275) ultimately Duplessis neglects to integrate the analogy with the male dominance for which twoness is also responsible. Therefore we understand that Janie, in flying by a sexist application of language, has once again transcended the influences of nationality.

[4]However, this is not to say that DuPlessis's observations are only useful to our discussion through what they lack: we will have noted that she points out other significant implications ([nets] of sexual inequality) of the Nietzchean 'slave mentality', in the 'rights of possessions, and sexual arousals enforced by wife-beating…' that constitute the men's 'self-proclaimed [power] substitute'.

Analysis

[1]The student indicates he is building on a critic (Bond's) idea about co-talking, but drawing a different conclusion to the critic. [2]Then he brings in another essay – by Duplessis, pointing out that her argument comes close to what he is trying to say, but his argument takes hers further. [3]He continues discussing her argument, but points out a flaw – for the student something is missing. Pointing out this missing thing helps him to express his own argument more clearly. [4]However, he does not simply critique Duplessis, he points out what is useful about her argument, to continue making his own, whilst showing he is not interested in simply rejecting other people's arguments out of hand, rather he is thinking about how he can use them to get the most useful, convincing interpretation of the book.

Use words precisely, acknowledging they can be ambiguous (see the
Defining your Terms section of this chapter)

Allow for complications and express your argument accordingly

---

Example essay

[1]Clearly this 'Universalisation of Western liberal democracy' (Fukuyama) and its accompanying values has not been totally straightforward. [2]There has been stubborn resistance by groups who have committed acts of pro-test ranging from peaceful demonstration to mass murder in the name of avoiding membership to the 'Enlightened' world. [3]Cahoone characterises the Khomeini-led Iranian revolution as the 'first major shock to the trium-phant liberal paradigm' (2005, p. 2). Faith in liberalism, however, increased in subsequent years, especially at the end of the Cold War, when liberal democracy 'triumphed' over communism and, in the eyes of theorists like Fukuyama, seemed to reign supreme as the most refined political mani-festation of the 'universal human desire for recognition and freedom', and the best political environment for the creation of an advanced society (Cahoone, 2005, pp. 9–10). [4]In the post-September the 11th world, how-ever, this self-congratulation now feels premature.

Analysis

[1]The student first points out the complication, grounding his argument with a key theorist – Fukuyama. [2]He then begins to illustrate the point with examples. [3]In so doing, he refers to another commentator, to continue thinking about the complicated situation, and the way it can be summa-rised. In this way, he sums up the main argument used by both Cahoone and Fukuyama. [4]Finally, however, he characterises their commentary as self-congratulation, giving an example of why the situation now needs to be viewed differently.

Demonstrate, through your own explanations, that you understand any theory you are using

Use the theory to analyse a text/situation/cultural product

Example essay

[1]We will look at some of the main themes of Neo-Platonism in order to ground any assertion of the consideration of the ceiling as a Neo-Platonic work. [2]The goal of Neo-Platonism, much like any religion, is the re-apprehension of the higher harmony of divine order (Saslow, 1991:30). The origins of this thought are found in Plato. He believed that the fundamental cure for the cultural problems found in Athenian society could be sought by the educated ruling classes through a life of dialectical philosophical practice. The final aim of this was to reach the "unhypothesized first principles," which were considered the starting points of virtue and rationality (Hankins, 1990:9).

Central to the ideas of Neo-Platonism (revived and expanded by Plotinus and others in the third century A.D.) is the concept that there is an indivisible and transcendant "One" which is outside the realm of being and not-being and is the foundation of all things. Implicit in the original passage from the 'unity' into the 'pluarity' is the "decline from the perfect to the imperfect" (Honour and Flemming, 1999: 220). In the mind of the Christian Neo-Platonist, this singular entity is of course God, and at the time of the Renaissance classical Platonic writing on this subject was seen to have foreshadowed the coming of Jesus. A hierarchy is therefore implied with the unified God at the top and the multiplicity of man at the bottom.

[3]One of the most striking Neo-Platonic features of the Sistine Chapel ceiling is therefore its hierarchic structure. The hierarchy runs both vertically from low to high and horizontally from the entrance to the altar end. In the vertical aspect, the first layer we see painted by Michelangelo shows the ancestors of Christ depicted in the lunettes.

Analysis

[1]First, the student introduces the reason for using the theory to help interpret the cultural product: Michelangelo's frescos on the Sistine Chapel ceiling. [2]He then goes on to outline the main tenets of Neo-Platonism, first using Saslow and Hankins to provide introduction and context, then identifying what is central to the theory and highlighting its relevance to the subject at hand. The quotations used are picked out judiciously to help the explanation remain clear and succinct. [3]Finally, the usefulness of the theory in an analysis of the frescos is made clear, the notion of hierarchy being the connecting factor between the two paragraphs.

Read between the lines
When reading, think about the agenda of the writer and consider how they are expressing their ideas

Consider this extract from a student's dissertation comparing British and American newspaper reactions to the bicentennial of the French Revolution.

Example essay

[1]Unlike several American journalists, several British writers do not concentrate on the actual character of the events on the 14th July 1789. Instead, they use the example of the Fall of the Bastille to demonstrate the exceptionally violent nature of the French Revolution. [2]The *Times*, commenting on the lack of Parisians at the celebrations on the 14th July 1989, argued that the reasons for this were obvious stating:

> The French are the most sophisticated people on the planet ... the last thing they want is to be reminded that a mere 200 years ago their great, great, great, great grandma was wandering around with somebody's head on a pole. (S. Pile, *Times*, 16 July, 1989)

This quotation showcases the violent and vulgar aspects of the Fall of the Bastille, purposely emphasising, but in a sense also trivialising the features not worthy of celebration. [3]The rest of the article also displays the belief that many French people did not see any point in the celebrations, as they did not want to be associated with the violence of the revolution. [4]The issue of violence is used by this British journalist, whose opinions are representative of a number of articles from right-leaning media outlets, to undermine the importance of the Revolution and the reasons for the enormous celebrations. These British writers conveniently leave out the fact that there was a reported three million spectators within France celebrating. Such one-sided journalism is an attack on the importance of the Revolution, reasons for celebrating the event, and the celebrations themselves.

Analysis

[1]This student shows he is thinking about how the newspaper articles are written, and what their agenda is. [2]He introduces the quotation from the *Times*, stating how he is reading it. After the quotation he provides an interpretation about how the article is expressed – in a manner which emphasises the vulgar, but also trivialises the revolution. [3]He puts this in the context of the rest of the article, [4]and then puts the article in the context of other 'right-leaning' articles. This leads to an opportunity to make the agenda clear by noting what has been missed out – the large attendance of French people at the celebrations. This helps him conclude the journalism is one-sided, the agenda to attack the importance of the Revolution.

Becoming a critic

Your degree is structured to help you develop the critical voice we have been thinking about in this section. Lectures are designed to give you a context about a subject, but also to get you to ask questions about the topic and develop your own ideas. In seminars you are encouraged to express your own ideas, but also listen to others and adjust what you think – the more prepared you are to contribute and respond thoughtfully to others, the more you will notice your own critical opinions growing.

Moreover, you will be encouraged to read a variety of materials, and think how other people present their own ideas, within the context of a wider debate. This reading should prepare you for your own writing, the written assignments at university being the real opportunity for you to develop your own set of questions, answers and complications about the topic.

Are you *reading* critically? Every time you read a secondary text, ask questions.

- What do I like about this?
- What is good about the ideas being presented?
- Are there any weaknesses with the ideas being shown?
- How does it compare to what I already know?
- What is the most convincing aspect of the argument being presented?
- Could any improvements be made to the ideas?
- How could I critically situate my ideas/opinions alongside this work?

Are you *writing* critically? Ask yourself,

- What does my question mean and do I understand what is required of me?
- Am I looking at this problem from many different angles?
- Have I paid close enough critical attention to all my sources?
- Can I reduce the crux of my argument to a single sentence or a short paragraph? (This shows you have got a clear overview of what you are thinking.)
- What is the most effective structure for my argument?
- Have I supported my argument with the strongest available evidence and reasons?
- Have I developed my argument logically, stage by stage, or have I merely written a narrative?
- Is my argument consistent, or does it contain internal contradictions?

● Summary

Learning how to write at university involves two main processes: working out what your tutors expect from you, and finding out how to develop your own knowledge and critical opinion of your subject. This chapter has provided guidelines for both of these processes but you must make sure you also pay great attention to the guidelines you receive from your tutors in the form of handbooks, online information and, of course, what they tell you in person. They will also spend time giving you feedback on your work which you should also pay continual attention to. The next chapter will build upon the information given here and outline some strategies for meeting your tutors' expectations. I will also suggest ways to structure and articulate your ideas effectively within an academic university environment and beyond.

5 Written Assignments 2: How to Approach your Essay

● Introduction

In Chapter 4 we started to think about what is expected of a university assignment. This chapter is designed to help you think about how you approach your written assignments. More than anything, you need to understand that, in two very important ways, writing *is a process*. Firstly, as we've already indicated, you don't arrive at university knowing how to write an undergraduate essay, you *learn* these skills over time. Secondly, writing any assignment involves a process in itself; you don't just sit down at your desk and begin writing your essay from scratch, beginning to end, in one go. This section aims to help you focus and so, perhaps, speed up this process, by going through some strategies to help you improve your writing, making sure you avoid some serious pitfalls, and thinking about how to tackle your largest writing project – the dissertation.

● The art of drafting

Writing is a process which takes time. It can be demoralising sitting in front of a blank computer screen planning to write your whole essay in one go. In fact, it is virtually impossible to produce an effective essay in one draft. You need to give yourself time to get your ideas on paper, link them up, work out what your argument is, make sure it is clearly written, ensure the conclusion is consistent with the introduction, and check that you have cited all of your sources.

What drafting style works for you?

There is no one, definitive approach for drafting a piece of written work. Different approaches work for different people: your first writing projects at university will give you the opportunity to figure out what methods work for you. I think it is fair to say that every writer is in a continual process of working out what planning and drafting style suits them. Some ideas you could try are:

1. Working out what the question is asking you to do: how do you interpret the question?
2. Planning the essay. Get your ideas down on paper. Planning an approach to essay writing might depend on essay length and the type of question, but you need to sort out what basic points you want to make: you may entirely agree with the question, disagree with it, or see that there are different ways of approaching the issue.
3. Producing a first draft in which you follow your plan and get as many ideas down as possible, prioritising getting your main points down.
4. Working with a draft to make sure you get the structure right and you are answering the question.
5. Fine-tuning the style – read the essay out to yourself and think about how it sounds. Give it to a friend to read.
6. Proofreading for the final time and making sure you have checked all the important presentation details such as spelling, punctuation, word count, information on front page, line spacing and referencing.

This list provides ideas which could work for you – but also suggests a linear order which may not be appropriate for your particular style of working.

Finding a system which works for you

A key process of learning to write effectively is finding a drafting system which works for you. This can take time – it is a process after all – but it is well worth thinking self-consciously about how you work best. Is it easier for you to have a thorough plan in place before beginning to write a draft? Can you only begin to start planning once you have started writing? Do you want to leave as much time as possible to perfect your style, or do you write slowly because you think carefully about every word? There is no right process – the only thing you should definitely make sure you do is *write more than one draft*. Or, at the very least, leave time to edit the draft you have written.

Do you have problems using a 'traditional' drafting process?

- Many people can only generate ideas by starting to write, so if you are finding it difficult to write a plan **you could start writing first and then devise a plan from your writing**.

- You may find it very difficult to write anything before you are absolutely certain of how your work will be structured. In this case, **you may want to get feedback on a detailed plan from your tutor or friends**.

- If producing writing which flows is a problem, **try producing one paragraph at a time, and then working on the links between paragraphs afterwards**. This can sometimes be a way to work out your argument. For example, it can be a good idea, when finding useful information in your reading to actually start writing a paragraph based around the ideas it sparks off, rather than only writing more fragmented notes.

- If you are finding it difficult to work out whether your piece of writing has a logical argument, **try summing up each paragraph in one sentence, set out the sentences as a flow chart and see if they follow through in a way which makes sense**.

- If you are trying one method of writing and it isn't working, don't waste time and energy walking down an unproductive path, **try another strategy**. For example, you may find yourself on a roll with writing and then suddenly run out of things to say. At this point, going back to your books, proofreading what you have written, and readjusting your plan are all ways to keep working and get your inspiration flowing again.

Things to remember

Your writing should end up seeming linear and polished, however many stages it has been through beforehand. **Give yourself time** to mess around with ideas and come up with an argument which is well thought through and convincing. Then, give yourself time to hone this argument down to a set of paragraphs that link effectively and form a logical thoughtful argument. You will always end up with ideas you cannot include in the final draft. These are not wasted; they are a necessary part of your thought process and could be used in seminar discussions. Even if you do not get to use them again they have been necessary for you to come to the ideas that will fit into the final essay.

● Developing an argument

Whatever the topic, an essay needs to present an argument, but putting together an argument takes time, effort and planning. How are you going to start? Everyone plans in different ways; you will be planning your essay's argument all the way through the research process, and most probably throughout the writing process as well. Here are some suggestions to help you start.

Start reading

Beginning to read around your topic will often spark ideas for further possible avenues of research. If you are reading the right sort of books – see the reading lists for the module – then you should be getting a feel for the territory. Try to work out what the main areas of academic focus have been; where there are disagreements in interpretation; where there are different schools of thought or criticism. The new vocabularies that you find in these books will probably seem quite alien or daunting at first. You might not be able to follow all of the arguments that you come across, or know to whom certain writers refer, or to whom they are responding. Don't let this put you off (unless you understand *none* of what they are writing about). Your familiarity with the ways of writing in your discipline, and your familiarity with some key thinkers or critics will become greater the more you read over the course of your degree. It may well take you until the end of your degree to become fully confident in reading these texts.

Use visual aids

You may find it helpful to keep a record of your thinking process, either by writing a list of how your main ideas connect, producing a spider diagram, or writing your main ideas for paragraphs on post-it notes which you can then move around when thinking about the most helpful structure for your essay.

Pursue possible avenues in your research

You may find that you need to start doing the research first to work out what the different sections of the essay will be. The important thing is to give yourself the space and time to think through and explain your argument. Once you have decided what material you need to cover you must make a decision about how you will analyse it.

Look at each of these essay questions and write in the boxes below the main points you think you should include in the essay. It doesn't matter if you don't know about the subject: think about how the question can be split up into smaller questions, issues which will need addressing, and terms which will need defining. See the Feedback section at the back of the book for some thoughts on these exercises (pp. 186–7).

Sample essay question 1
Tyrant or Founder of Europe? To what extent does Charlemagne deserve the esteem that has been heaped upon him?

Sample essay question 2
'Although made in Germany, Tom Tykwer's *Run Lola Run* is hardly a German film'. Discuss.

(Our thanks go to Professor Paul Cooke for this example.)

● Building up your argument paragraph by paragraph

You need to build up your argument step by step, using each paragraph to build on the points from the last one. Paragraphs are the building blocks of an essay and the more you concentrate on making each one present a coherent point in a clear, structured way, whilst linking to the last one, the better your essay will be.

Each paragraph within an essay should have a single main theme, point or argument. Begin a new paragraph every time you introduce a new theme, point or argument. Closely linked sub-themes, points and arguments may also be included within the same paragraph. When you look at a paragraph, you should be able to sum it up in a single short statement.

Each paragraph should contain:

- the 'topic sentence' – the main theme, point or argument should be stated in the first sentence. This sentence announces the topic but it should also make a transition from the previous paragraph.
- supporting material – which could involve: providing a brief history of the topic specified in the topic sentence; developing the argument of the topic statement, stating the reasoning behind the argument of the topic sentence; introducing examples to support and/or challenge the argument of the topic sentence (which could take the form of facts, statistics, quotations, brief anecdotes, etc.). Evaluate the supporting material: compare or contrast sources; analyse causes and reasons; examine effects and consequences; discuss issues raised etc; discuss one or more of the topic sentence's key terms. Explain any unclear terms.
- concluding sentences – any conclusions should be drawn at the very end of the paragraph. Your concluding sentence should ideally link back to the topic sentence, and possibly to the following paragraph. You may find that there is no need to provide a concluding sentence.

Length of paragraphs
Be careful that your paragraphs are not too long or too short. A single sentence is not a paragraph: the argument in the topic sentence will need to be developed and supported with evidence. Conversely, if you bundle a lot of material into a single paragraph it gives the impression you do not have control over your subject. If a paragraph appears to be too long, look to see if there is more than one major theme, point or argument in it. If there is, separate them into two or more paragraphs.

EXERCISE

Look at the passage of writing below and consider:

Where should the writer have begun a new paragraph?
What would be the main point of each paragraph?

To the question "What is Marxist criticism?" it may be tempting to respond with another question: "What does it matter?" In light of the rapid and largely unanticipated demise of Soviet-style communism in the former USSR and throughout Eastern Europe, it is understandable to suppose that Marxist literary analysis would disappear too, quickly becoming an anachronism in a world enamored with full-market capitalism. In fact, however, there is no reason why Marxist criticism should weaken, let alone disappear. It is, after all, a phenomenon distinct from Soviet and Eastern European communism, having had its beginnings nearly eighty years before the Bolshevik revolution and having thrived since the 1940s, mainly in the West – not as a form of communist propaganda but rather as a form of critique, a discourse for interrogating all societies and their texts in terms of certain specific issues. Those issues – including race, class, and the attitudes shared within a given culture – are as much with us as ever, not only in contemporary Russia but also in the United States. The argument could even be made that Marxist criticism has been strengthened by the collapse of Soviet-style communism. There was a time, after all, when few self-respecting Anglo-American journals would use Marxist terms or models, however illuminating, to analyze Western issues or problems. It smacked of sleeping with the enemy. With the collapse of the Kremlin, however, old taboos began to give way. Even the staid *Wall Street Journal* now seems comfortable using phrases like "worker alienation" to discuss the problems plaguing the business world.

T. Eagleton, 'Marxist Criticism', in E. Brontë, ed. by L.H. Peterson, *Wuthering Heights, Case Studies in Contemporary Criticism*, 2nd edn (Basingstoke: Palgrave Macmillan, 2003).

Our feedback is on p. 187; did you agree with us?

Note: this example is taken from published work. You are not expected to produce work of such a high standard, but you can learn from the good scholarly practices it demonstrates.

● Introductions and conclusions

Introductions and conclusions are perhaps the most important parts of an essay and certainly the most difficult sections to write. This is because they play a number of different roles, as well as being your first and final word on the subject. Let us deal with introductions first of all.

Beginning to write the introduction

You may find yourself struggling to write an introduction simply because you are starting with a blank page in front of you. Try to avoid this by work-ing from a plan, from which you should have some idea of what you will include in the introduction. If you give yourself time to draft, then you can begin by writing a working introduction, in which you include the main ten-ets of your argument but then go back when re-drafting and hone the intro-duction more to what you have actually written in the body of the essay. In this way, the introduction becomes both the first thing and the last thing you will write.

What should an introduction do?

Introduce your argument

First of all, you need to remember that the introduction is there to introduce your argument, not the whole subject. It is easy to become overwhelmed when writing an introduction and begin to write overly generalised com-ments about a topic in an attempt to demonstrate more knowledge than you actually have or need to have. This can produce statements which are not useful, often meaningless, and likely to irritate your marker.

Indicate you understand the essay question and how you are interpreting it

No essay question can be approached from one angle only, and many are designed to be open enough to be answered in multiple ways. It is therefore important that you let your marker know what you understand the essay question to mean, and how you have decided to approach your response. This can be done effectively by re-phrasing the question in your own words, and by talking your reader through some of the main issues the question raises, leading them to a series of statements outlining how you will tackle these issues.

Establish what you will be arguing and how

Perhaps the most important role of an introduction is to establish for the reader the main drive and logic of your argument. Whilst it is important

---

to indicate how you will construct this argument, this does not mean you should make too many statements telling your reader how to write an essay (e.g. 'then I will outline the main arguments for and against...', 'then I will conclude'). It is rather that you should tell your reader what you are actually going to say; for example, 'I will therefore show that so-and-so is right.', 'As will be demonstrated, whilst the situation seems to be this ... this is equally integral.'

Locate your argument in a critical debate/historical context

Whilst the role of an introduction is to launch *your* argument, it is most effective when given within the context of the critical debate with which you are engaging in the essay. Depending on your subject this could work in different ways. For example, in History it may be useful to provide the historical context for the particular events you are writing about; for English literature you may want to indicate the main approaches critics of the texts have taken; for Cultural Studies it may be most appropriate to outline the context of the theoretical approach with which you are engaging.

Begin to define the key terms of the essay

Many Arts and Humanities essay topics involve using words and theories which can be utilised in a number of ways. It helps your reader, lets you demonstrate your own understanding more thoroughly and allows your writing to be more precise, if you indicate how you are engaging with particular theories and how you are using certain terms.

EXERCISE   **Example introductions for you to consider**

In this exercise we have given you examples of four introductions.

Read through the first – from a published monograph (academic single-authored book) – and take note of the places, signalled in **bold**, in which the writer introduces the main topic for discussion, locates his argument within a critical debate, introduces his argument, and discusses his methodology. Although this introduction is wider-ranging and more sophisticated than the ones you will be expected to produce in your degree – it is from a book after all – it shows that academic writers practise what they preach, demonstrating how useful an introduction can be in indicating what the argument of the work will be, and how this argument will be made.

[The author introduces the main topic for discussion.] The French blackmailer-*libellistes* operating out of London between 1758 and 1792 were involved in one of the most shadowy and, in the eyes of the Bourbon government, most criminal and dangerous, aspects of a vast and influential international clandestine publishing industry. Their publications were among the most scandalous political texts of the eighteenth century. [He then **locates the argument within a critical debate.**] In recent years, such works have attracted considerable attention from historians, many of whom stress the central role of scurrilous pamphlets in undermining the monarchy and covering leading political figures in contempt, above all Louis XV and Louis XVI's queen, Marie-Antoinette. It has even been suggested that such pamphlets had a greater role in revolutionary causation than leading enlightenment thinkers such as Montesquieu, whose writings empowered opposition under the monarchy, or Rousseau, who so inspired egalitarian Jacobin politicians such as Robespierre and the militant, artisanal *sans culottes*. [**The author indicates the implications of critical debate.**] Thus scandalous pamphleteering has been heavily implicated in the origins of the French revolution of 1789. [**He then makes a direct statement indicating his argument and methodology, and notes its originality, and so its place within critical debate.**] Nevertheless, this monograph offers the first collective study of the *libellistes*, their works, and their significance. In the process, it radically revises existing perceptions of the role of gutter pamphlets, pamphleteers, 'political pornography', and clandestine pamphleteering under the late *ancien régime* (ie. pre-revolutionary period). It contends that the social origins, career paths, and motives of the *libellistes* have been misunderstood; their political role and influence misread; the nature of their pamphlets misconstrued; and their wider political significance largely overlooked. To appreciate the *libellistes*' significance, however, it is first necessary to consider how *ancien régime* French politics functioned and the current state of historical thinking about scandalous pamphleteering and the origins of the French revolution. This is the main purpose of this introductory chapter.

Simon Burrows, *Blackmail, Scandal, and Revolution: London's French Libellistes, 1758–1792* (Manchester: MUP, 2006).

The next three introductions are from students' essays. It would be useful for you to read them, and consider whether they seem effective. Do they fulfil the expectations outlined above? What do you think they do well? What do they not do so well? You can compare your ideas about this to our commentary at the back of the book.

Essay entitled: 'Othello's Fatal Flaw: The Erroneous Belief of Narrative Control'

There are many reasons people tell stories. They are an entertaining and useful way to convey information, and indeed moral messages. They may be commissioned by an audience and can be used to satisfy curiosity. The focus, however, may lie more heavily upon the storyteller and their rhetorical skills. More sinister motivations may also be at play; the storyteller may have someone particular in mind they wish to hear the story or, indeed, to whom they are referring in the story. The story then becomes more than a fictional process and the storyteller or narrator, as well as the listener, can be seen to play a more active role in the story itself, becoming character as well as reporter. This role of storyteller/ character is further problematised if the person one is creating and relating a fiction for, is oneself. A problem that can be immediately identified with this particular scenario is the consideration of to what extent the storyteller then becomes inextricably intertwined with the *fiction* and loses sight of the fact that it is a narrative process rather than a fixed and universal reality. This is what Stephen Greenblatt suggests could be happening to the character of Othello in Shakespeare's tragedy of the same name. He writes of 'a Borges-like narrative that is forever constituting itself out of the materials of the present instant, a narrative in which the storyteller is constantly swallowed up by the story' (238).

In this play storytelling plays a very important role in the construction and ultimate destruction of Othello's identity. Iago, Othello's ancient, is of course generally seen to be the main manipulator and the main 'storyteller' within the text, but I do not think he could progress as far as he does within his manipulation and deceit without the additional help he receives from the other characters' strong inclinations to dramatising, romanticising and idealising to

Exercise continued

the extent of fictionalising their own lives. In this essay I would like to consider the extent to which Othello, himself, is guilty of this kind of 'narrative self-fashioning' (Greenblatt, 238) whilst also examining reasons why he may be prone to such self-romanticisation and the consequences of indulging (however unwittingly) such an inclination.

References: Stephen Greenblatt, *Renaissance Self-Fashioning* (Chicago and London: University of Chicago Press, 1980).

Essay question entitled: 'When the soul of a man is born in this country, there are nets flung at it to hold it back from flight. You talk to me of nationality, language, religion. I shall try to fly by those nets [i.e. fly past them, escape them].' James Joyce, *A Portrait of the Artist as a Young Man* (1916). Discuss attitudes to any one or two of these 'nets' (nationality, language, religion) in either *Dubliners* or *Their Eyes Were Watching God*.

"Us colored folks is too envious of one 'nother. Dat's how come us don't git no further than us do. Us talks about de white man keepin' us down! Shucks! He don't have tuh. Us keeps our own selves down." (Hurston, p. 63)

Lee Coker's wise words to his friend Amos Hicks describe the trend that will be exposed over the course of this essay: that the 'nets' in Zora Neale Hurston's *Their Eyes Were Watching God* are often flung in confusion by the very characters they entangle. African Americans become caught up trying to escape from issues of nationality they have unwittingly created themselves, influenced by the adverse racial conditions they find themselves in (distinguishing between those who truly find themselves and those who fail to fly by). We will see how Hurston lets Janie transcend some of the problems she faces using traditional Negro language play, a step of 'crucial importance ... as the signifying practice in and through which the subject is made into a social being' (Kaplan, p.72), while examination of others' use of the same conventions (of signifying) will demonstrate that even these seemingly free forms of self-expression can become self-destructive weapons when influenced by the identity crises that derive from conflicting split nationality.

Reference: Cora Kaplan, 'Language and Gender' in *Sea Changes: Culture and Feminism* (Norfolk: Thetford, 1986).

Exercise continued

Essay entitled: 'Moral relativism is incoherent, because it insists on the one hand that morality is relative, and on the other hand, that we have a non-relative moral obligation to be tolerant of other people and cultures.' Discuss.

Moral relativism was a concept made popular in the later nineteenth century when anthropologists partly subsidized by colonizing governments began learning more about the nature and status of so-called 'primitive' peoples. Many anthropologists eventually reacted against the imperialism of their governments and viewed the peoples they studied as intelligent men and women whose views should be treated equally to their own.

This shows that moral relativism was born out of two premises. Firstly, societies have been discovered which had contrasting norms and mores. Secondly, the people in these societies deserved respect and their morals should be taken seriously.

The argument viewed in its simplest form and as seen in the essay title states that different moral standards are correct for different people. We have to recognise at this stage that this view of moral relativism is not simply saying that different people believe that different moral standards are correct for them, it states that different moral standards are actually correct for different people.

Conclusions

Conclusions can also be tricky to write; you want them to finish your argument effectively and it is tempting, again, to do this by trying to sum up the whole topic. Again, make sure you stay within the scope of what you know and can be expected to know, whilst pointing your reader to some interesting ways of thinking about the topic. There are a few things you should try to do with your conclusion.

Sum up the main strands of your argument

Here you have the opportunity to remind your reader of why they should be convinced about your argument: this means summing it up in an effective way which reiterates the main points. It is difficult to do this in a way which does not come across as repetitive; you should not worry about repeating the same points, but at the same time it is good to try and think of different ways of expressing them, perhaps using different examples or indicating the wider implications of what you are saying.

Refer back to the main points of the essay question and be consistent with your introduction

This point is vital: it is imperative that your conclusion backs up and does not contradict your introduction. Markers often compare the two when making sure you have made a logical and consistent argument. It is a useful exercise when reading through a draft of your conclusion to go back to the essay question and your introduction and make sure you have covered the points the two raise. It can sometimes be helpful in an essay to refer back to questions/issues raised in the introduction and re-address them in the conclusion in light of the arguments you have developed throughout.

Clearly establish a point, or position (which could be quite complex), reiterating the evidence which justifies this position

Your conclusion should leave your reader in no doubt as to where you stand on a subject. It is easy to fall into the trap of writing a kind of 'on the one hand, on the other' conclusion, which leaves the reader to decide what they think. This can undermine all kinds of interesting points and arguments you may have made in the main body of your essay. Good university writing is about making confident decisions, even on subjects which seem almost insurmountably complex. However complex, a conclusion needs to be reached which follows from the main evidence presented in your essay. You could perhaps end up coming up with a series of conclusions – a number of useful ways of thinking about a text, or a conclusion which utilises the framework of a particular theoretical approach. The important thing is that you do bring the main points of your argument together into a conclusion.

EXERCISE   Example conclusions for you to consider

In this exercise we have given you examples of four conclusions.

Read through the first – from a published monograph (academic single-authored book) – and take note of the places, signalled in **bold**, in which the writer sums up the main strands of the argument, hints at the wider implications of the essay's main argument, and refers to points made in the introduction but looks at them in a renewed way. Although this conclusion is wider-ranging and more sophisti- cated than the ones you will be expected to produce in your degree – it is from a book after all – it shows that academic writers practise what they preach, demonstrating how effective a conclusion can be in reminding the reader of the most important parts of the argument,

Exercise continued

whilst thinking about the further implications of this argument, and pointing to how the essay should have helped the reader understand the situation in a new, convincing way.

> **[The author sums up the main strands of the argument and clearly establishes a complex position.]** These, then, are some of the ways in which the notion of an unconscious has come to have an impact on literary theory, philosophy, anthropology, and linguistics. At least, these are some of the ways that psychoanaly- sis has chosen to use such disciplines as a way of describing what is by definition indescribable: the unknowable part of the psyche and its activities which the term "unconscious" stands in for. We have noted that, because the unconscious is an abstraction, an invisible "place" in the mind, or an unseeable system of energy flowing beyond consciousness, it is then condemned to being rep- resented concretely through analogies and extended metaphors. **[She hints at wider implications/debates of main points made in essay.]** But perhaps the converse is also true. Perhaps the unconscious is the way in which we imagine the unknowable and its hidden workings. Is it possible, then, that the "unconscious" is the twentieth century version of the mythologies humankind always generates to explain the inexplicable, to chart the "unknown ter- rain" which ultimately remains mysterious in (and to) the psyche? It may be that when we discuss or describe the unconscious, we are revealing more about the human will to explore and explain precisely that which is unknowable and inexplicable than we are about any system or topography of the mind. **[The author refers back to the main points made in the introduction and consid- ers them in a new way.]** To return to the idea which opened this essay, any discussion of the unknowable must perforce be born of the known, and therefore be nothing more than speculation. And yet, it may be that the way we speculate about the unknown will tell us in itself about the structures and patterns of the psyche, about its limitations and prejudices.

> Françoise Meltzer, 'Unconscious' in Lentricchia, Frank and McLaughlin, Thomas (eds), *Critical Terms for Literary Study* (Chi- cago and London: University of Chicago Press, 1990), p. 162.

The next three conclusions are from students' essays. It would be useful for you to read them, and consider whether they seem effective. Do they fulfil the expectations outlined above? What do you think they do well? What do you think they do not do so well? You can compare your ideas about this to our feedback at the back of the book.

From an essay entitled: 'Othello's Fatal Flaw: The Erroneous Belief of Narrative Control'

Terry Eagleton asserts that:

> Othello lives straight out an imaginary self-image, his being indissociable from rhetoric and theatricality ... he starts off with a wholly 'imaginary' reality: his rotund, mouthfilling rhetoric signifies a delusory completeness of being, in which the whole world becomes a signified obediently reflecting back the imperious signifier of the self. (Eagleton, 69)

Whilst I believe he is pushing the idea of Othello's fictionality to the extreme, he is right to point to the theatricality and narcissistic tendencies of the title character's entire being. Othello is introduced to the audience at the beginning of the play as a proud soldier, who has travelled and is happy to entertain, inform, provoke pity, be accepted into society because of his story-telling and willingness to play that particular role. Throughout the play his self-image is threatened and he becomes swept along by manipulations of his own story, which he fatally tries to create and control. Unfortunately it is too late before he realises that in reality nobody can 'narrate' their own lives because the characters in each person's own story are all the central figures in stories of their own.

Reference: Terry Eagleton, *William Shakespeare* (Oxford: Blackwell, 1986).

From a history essay entitled: How successful were the anthropological methods of Mass Observation in offering sources in exploring the culture of drinking in 1930s Bolton?

In conclusion, it would appear the anthropological methods used do seem in part to be a success as they provide some form of exploration about Bolton's drinking culture. The methods of observation, which are used frequently within the study, provide an historian with an insight into what people did in the pubs in Bolton. Furthermore, the methods of direct and indirect interviewing obtained the views and opinions of individuals, which would have been difficult to extract through any other methods. The anthropological methods did, however, have several flaws. There does not seem to be any regulating book or authority which meant the panellists who used these methods, must have had a variation of approaches in gathering their information. This would make it difficult to compare the findings objectively and come to final conclusions. Also, the human condition dictates that anthropological methods such as observation do not provide solid evidence that an event happened as it had been reported in an eye-witness report, as people recollect incidents in different ways. Another issue that needs to be taken into consideration when examining these sources is the left-leaning agenda the Mass-Observation group were intent on pursuing. This meant there was a concentration on the working class, which dictated that a complete analysis of people from different social classes in Bolton was not achievable. But despite these apparent flaws, it is difficult to find a better method of exploring Bolton's drinking culture in the 1930s. A more ideal method would have been by using surveillance tapes and studying the results from the footage. Unfortunately such extensive camera footage collection was not produced in the 1930s so this method was not then possible. In addition, people can act differently when they know cameras are watching them. So it would seem the anthropological methods used were probably the best methods available for exploring Bolton's drinking culture. Even though these methods cannot be used as conclusive evidence they do provide a partially successful exploration of Bolton's drinking culture in the 1930s.

Exercise continued

From an essay entitled: 'Tony Blair, Intercultural Communication and Universal Values'

In conclusion, using Habermas' analysis, we have seen that the use of values as a strategic tool of power is at odds with the communicative manner in which universal values must be formed. Universal values should ultimately be formed through a discourse which involves all those who are going to adopt them. It is pointless to try to impose unilaterally our values on any dissenting culture, since universal values must be formed through agreement rather than imposition. If a fixed set of values is used strategically in order to achieve preordained results then this makes meaningful discourse with different and conflicting cultures even more unlikely. Blair's promotion of values serves only to strengthen his position with his domestic audience and if he wishes to engage fruitfully with a foreign one he will have to be prepared to discuss and compromise.

Feeling ambitious?

As we have seen from the examples in the exercises, introductions and conclusions can be written in many different ways. The most sophisticated ones really try to find an original but effective way to introduce and sum up the main argument – and so persuade the reader that it is well thought through and convincing. For example, with introductions it is not always most effective to simply say 'this essay will argue', or to begin with some generalised comment about the topic. The best introductions find a more subtle way to introduce the thought process behind the argument which will be made. This can be through the close reading of a useful passage from an academic or creative text; it could be through the analysis of some key data. This is how a fellow lecturer once put it to me:

I want quieter variations of the traditional opening lines: so, I don't much like 'in this essay I shall be arguing' and I really don't like 'the period' in a big clunky way. I like students to find tight textual moments that encapsulate their argument with a tiny detail; the preferable introductory line, then, to come at the end of the introduction and introduce the argument may be more along the lines of 'and this is indicative of the way the whole poem works', and this provides the perfect analogy for the [insert subject of discussion].

If possible, a good conclusion should hint at possible wider implications/ debates beyond the remit of the essay – establish wider relevance. Although it is not appropriate to bring into the conclusion key points which you have not mentioned before, it can be effective to get your reader to consider the ways in which your argument can impact upon the larger critical debate.

● Using quotations effectively

The way you incorporate quotations from primary and secondary material into your work can really affect what you are trying to argue. Try to avoid using long quotations, unless strictly necessary, and always justify the use of any you use. You can justify your choice by making sure you demonstrate how it fits into the context of your argument. A quotation might support a point you are making or it might function as the basis of a disagreement: for example, 'Although X says...', 'it is clear from the evidence in TEXT Y, that...'.

You need to make clear why each quotation is necessary and what you are doing with it. Never abandon a quotation: you must always address what you quote. If you are quoting from primary material (examples could include a fictional or poetic text, a historical source or a philosophical argument), make it clear how you are interpreting the quoted text, and what it is demonstrating. If you are quoting from secondary material (examples could include material used to comment on primary material such as theory, critical material, text books, historical monographs), make clear what your stance is in relation to the material quoted. For example, do you agree with it? Is a particularly controversial opinion being expressed? Are you using the quotation as an example of an idea which comes from a particular critical field? Do not use quotations from secondary texts merely to say what you would have explained in your own words. Secondary texts only convey opinions, not original evidence, so always treat them critically.

The following example is taken from published work. You are not expected to produce work of such a high standard but you can learn from the good scholarly practices it demonstrates.

Although tracing Spock's actual effects upon either parents' child-rearing techniques or their children's subsequent behaviour is impossible, his audience clearly took his views to heart. A marketing survey commissioned by Pocket Books reported that 40% of those responding referred to *Baby and Child Care* between two and four times per month, and that nearly one-third of those who owned *Baby and Child Care* consulted it oftener than once a week. "I simply live by my book," proclaimed one respondent. "*Baby and Child Care* is my closest friend," confided another.

Spock downplayed his influence. "My critics confuse the popularity of *BCC* with the book's influence," he claimed. "It is popular because it is cheap, complete and friendly. But in the few areas of child care in which I've really tried to change things, I haven't made a dent." Yet the evidence suggests otherwise, that Spock's advocacy could and did affect behaviour. Spock supported breast-feeding when few others did; breast-feeding assumed a more prominent role in popular literature about child rearing in the early 1950s after publication of *Baby and Child Care*. When Spock went against conventional wisdom and supported the use of pacifiers, he received a flood of letters from grateful mothers. Spock may not have been omnipotent. But "as the nation's unofficial godfather" ... he was clearly an authority with which to be reckoned.

Jane F. Levey, 'Spock, I Love Him', *Colby Quarterly*, 4, XXXVI (December 2000), p. 278.

Notice in this passage how the writer comments on the material she quotes in the process of citing it, incorporating it into her own argument about Spock's influence. Consider how she uses the statistical evidence at the beginning to counteract Spock's opinion of his own influence, presenting a thought-provoking analysis of the situation which makes clear her reasoning.

The way you place the quotation within your argument is also important. Here are some useful phrases you might use to *introduce* quotations:

As X points out,...
According to Y...
To quote from Z, '...'
Burrows suggests that...
Hargreaves shows us that...
Referring to ..., Marx argues that
As Chomsky argued...
In *The Republic*, Plato's primary argument is...

Whilst acknowledging ... Freud makes the significant claim that ...
Writing in 1926, Woolf argued that ...

and some useful phrases to *follow* quotations:

However, Bates suggests that...
Yet this does not go far enough...
This seems untenable because...
This theory best fits the known facts, since...

● Avoiding plagiarism

Your academic work will involve reading, thinking about, and responding critically to *other* people's work. Your essays and assignments will therefore quite legitimately include references to other works and discussions of the material found in them. It is good academic practice to read, comment upon, criticise and cite the work of other authors: it demonstrates your understanding of the field, your knowledge of the key thinkers and concepts, and shows that you have a sophisticated and confident grasp of the issues at hand. A piece of work which did not refer to any other work would not look like a serious piece of academic writing. In responding to and referencing other people's work you are not only protecting yourself from accusations of plagiarism, but you are demonstrating that you are developing your skills as an academic in your own right.

What you *must* do is distinguish between your *own* work, ideas, criticisms and arguments and those of the author/s that you have come across in your reading. This is of paramount importance, because failure to reference correctly may mean that you are presenting that person's work as your own.

> Find out how your university defines plagiarism.

Ways to avoid plagiarising

A good way to ensure against accidental plagiarism is through organising your note-taking properly. Imagine that you are writing an essay and you review the notes that you have written earlier in the semester. Have you made it absolutely clear where, when and why you took these notes? Were they taken during a lecture? Were they preparation for a seminar or tutorial? Were they from a book or a journal? If from a book, were they direct quotations or have you paraphrased or summarised the argument?

Now imagine that you have found some of your notes on a relevant topic, and in the margin you have written the name of the author and the name of the book. It appears as though you have summarised one of the author's points, but you cannot be absolutely sure that it is not a direct quotation. As you are not sure, you have to go back to the library and find the book and the page and the quote. What a waste of time: this could have been avoided with a bit of careful organisation. You need to develop a method for identifying, quickly and easily, your own work from other people's work, to make sure you do not accidentally plagiarise. Here are some tips that you could use in your own note-taking.

- Use different colours, or perhaps symbols and different types of brackets, to distinguish between paraphrases/summaries/quotes and your own thoughts. Stick to this rule throughout your course.
- When note-taking always make sure you enclose your direct quotes in quotation marks.
- Indent large quotes as you would in your final essay.
- After you have used a paraphrase/summary/quote in your notes, include a box entitled 'What do I think about this?' and make sure you keep this separate from the quote itself.
- Always write out the whole reference during note-taking, including page number – this will save you lots of time!
- If you are making notes on a computer, write out the whole reference as it would appear in your bibliography/footnote. Then you can copy and paste this at a later stage of your essay writing.
- If you are photocopying from books or collections, photocopy the title page as this will include important information and will save you time.

Using and citing sources

There are several ways in which you might need to use sources as part of your own work. The University of Leeds plagiarism website identifies three ways, outlined below, where extra care is needed. It is important to show where you have found your ideas and distinguish these from your own work.

1. Paraphrasing

As the University of Leeds' plagiarism website says, you are paraphrasing when "[t]he author's original words are substantially rewritten, but the original meaning is retained" ('Plagiarism – University of Leeds Guide', University of Leeds, http://www.ldu.leeds.ac.uk/plagiarism/how.php [accessed 22/05/09]).

Paraphrasing someone else's work without acknowledging that this is what you have done still counts as presenting their work as your own. If you are paraphrasing then this cannot be the output of your *own* response to an issue – you are merely putting together someone else's work in a different way and using different words. This might, of course, be what you have been asked to do, and it might be necessary to demonstrate that you have understood a particular point, but be careful! Paraphrased sections of someone else's work must be referenced in full. You should also make it absolutely clear to the reader where your paraphrasing ends and where your critical analysis begins. A good way of doing this is to keep the paraphrased section and the analysis in separate paragraphs and *signpost* that this is what you have done. Again, poor note-taking might result in a paraphrased section of someone else's work being included in your own essay without acknowledgement.

2. Summarising

You are summarising when "[t]he author's original words are rewritten into a substantially shortened form that captures the most important elements" ('Plagiarism – University of Leeds Guide', University of Leeds, http://www.ldu.leeds.ac.uk/plagiarism/how.php [accessed 22/05/09]).

Again, summarising can be a useful and worthwhile academic activity, but it is important that you make absolutely clear where in your essay you are summarising and also the source which you have used. Summaries must therefore be referenced in full. You must also distinguish between your summary and your critical analysis of it. Again, as with paraphrasing, a good way of doing this is by keeping the summary and the analysis in separate paragraphs and *signpost* that this is what you have done.

3. Quotations

Students are often keen to include quotations in their work in order to demonstrate their breadth or depth of reading. This is understandable, but there are several pitfalls to look out for, and some common errors to try and avoid. Remember: secondary sources are not 'evidence'; you need to incorporate any quotation within your own critical argument. All quotations should be referenced in full. See **Using quotations effectively** on p. 109.

How to refer to the titles of different kinds of sources

When you refer to titles of works you should observe the following conventions:

- **Titles of books** should be in italics. This convention allows you to distinguish, for example, Hamlet the character from *Hamlet* the play.

● **Titles of short poems**, and **articles** from journals or **collections of essays** are conventionally given within inverted commas. So you would write about Wordsworth's *The Prelude*, but about Wordsworth's 'Hart-Leap Well'; Eliot's *Four Quartets*, but Eliot's 'Journey of the Magi'.
● **Titles of whole published works** such as films, journals, newspapers, CD-ROMs and television broadcasts should be in italics.

Collaboration and working in study groups

In some modules you will be asked to work as a group and come up with a piece of work to which you have all contributed. It is extremely important that you clarify with your tutor what he/she is expecting from your assignment – is it just one piece of written work for the whole group, or does each member have to come up with their own report/essay? Always make sure you know what the requirements are, and if there is any confusion at all, **ask your tutor**.

At other times you may find it helpful to work as part of a **study group**, to bounce ideas around, to help you clarify your own understanding or simply just to inspire one another. This is fine and can be a good way of learning (academics do this too), but you need to make sure that you are using your **own words** when it comes to writing your essays and assignments. Borrowing your friend's essay and paraphrasing sections from it is an academic offence – even if your friend has given you permission to use it. It still counts as plagiarism because you are presenting someone else's work as your own – even if you have 'substantially re-written' it.

Do I have to come up with completely original ideas?

Some students worry that they are being asked to come up with completely new answers to essay/exam questions – answers which have never been suggested or even *thought of* before. They worry that they could be accused of plagiarism if they have, by coincidence, come to the same conclusion as someone else (of whom they may never have heard). There is no need to worry, however. Tutors are looking for your *own* response to a question: what they want to see is that you have thought critically about the issue, read the appropriate sources and come to your own conclusions about them. Of course, someone else may have already come to the same conclusion as you, but by demonstrating your critical skills in your essay, you will show that your engagement with the question is uniquely your own. As long as you are presenting your own ideas, thoughts, criticisms, counter-criticisms phrased using sentences that you have composed, then you will have nothing to worry about.

Referencing systems

Referencing systems can seem confusing. For starters, there is more than one basic system (in fact, there are upwards of four!). If you do not know which one you should be using then consult your Departmental Handbook, which will probably include examples, or ask your tutor.

Remember that if you are a **Joint Honours** or **Elective** student, you may have to learn more than one referencing method, depending on the discipline of the module that you are studying. If in any doubt ask your tutor. Your library will have resources to help too.

The main referencing systems are:

- **MLA Referencing System (or *Author-Date System*)**
  Modern languages/linguistic and social sciences students might find that they are asked to use this system
- **MHRA Referencing System (or *Footnotes System*)**
  Humanities students might find that they are asked to use this system
- **Harvard Referencing System (or *Parentheses System*)**
  This system is used widely
- **Numeric Referencing System**
  Science students might find that they are asked use this system

● Proofreading

Proofreading, involving checking the presentation of the essay, the spelling, the punctuation, the grammar and syntax, is a vital part of the whole essay writing process. It can be easy to run out of time to proofread properly; try not to do this because even spending half an hour checking through your work can allow you to make significant, beneficial changes and demonstrate to your tutor that you approach your work carefully AND take your work seriously.

How to proofread

- **Find a place to concentrate.** Ensure you are in an environment in which you can concentrate fully, with no distractions.
- **Seek out others to help.** As with drafting, it may also be helpful to ask a friend to look through your work; being familiar with your work you may see what you want to see or what you think is there, not noticing typing errors (typos) or unclear passages which someone else will see.

● **Take advantage of your computer's proofreading functions.** Bear in mind that Microsoft™ Word™ and other word processors are designed to help with the proofreading process. They have a spelling and grammar check function, which is useful to use in the final check through. Ensure the language is set to UK English rather than US English, otherwise it will highlight some correctly spelt words as incorrect. Be questioning of the grammar function as it will sometimes make suggestions for rewrites of sentences which are unnecessary. If you realise you have made the same mistake throughout the essay, or you know you often make a certain kind of mistake (for example, a word you always spell incorrectly), then you could use the 'find and replace' function.

● **Read out loud.** This can really help identify mistakes and see where your writing could be more clear. Software such as Texthelp® can read out your text for you; ask your university computer services about acquiring this, as it can make a very useful proofreading tool.

Proofread for one thing at a time

You don't want proofreading to be an *endless* process, but you want to give enough time to it so that you really think about what you have written: whether you have clarified your argument, and whether you have caught all the typos and spelling mistakes. It can be useful, then, to read it through with different agendas, such as:

1. Your argument – Is it made clearly? Are there any sections which could be explained more precisely?
2. Your style – Is it consistent? Does it present your ideas in the best light? Does it sound fluid when read out loud?
3. Errors – Have you corrected all typos and spelling mistakes? Have you referenced correctly?

If you try reading for all three of these issues at the same time then you are bound to miss something. Read three times, each time bearing in mind one main issue, and you will produce a polished piece of work which does justice to your ideas.

● Dissertations and longer projects

A dissertation is a long research project which presents original research on a particular topic. It usually consists of a few chapters, or sections, and is your chance to really investigate an area of interest. Dissertations are usually undertaken in the final year of a degree, since they require you to use the research skills and enthusiasm/knowledge of the subject you have been building up throughout your time at university. They usually begin with a hypothesis – a theory about a specific subject – which is then put to the test through research. This means that in your dissertation you need to explain your hypothesis, and reasoning behind it, outline the research methods you have used to test it out, demonstrate how you undertook your research, write up your findings, and then discuss your conclusions. These different stages will be discussed in more detail below.

Note – a dissertation is a discussion

The term 'dissertation' originally used to mean 'an extended written treatment of a subject'. Dissertation comes from a Latin word 'dissertare' = 'to debate'. So, a dissertation is a discussion involving different points of view or sets of ideas. A dissertation will therefore not only examine a subject but will review different points of view about that subject.

Choosing a dissertation topic

Some departments will provide you with a list of possible topics, or subject areas suitable for a dissertation – others will ask you to write a proposal outlining your own particular research interest. Either way, choosing a topic can be tricky; you want to pick something you will be interested in, and also something with enough scope to withstand substantial investigation, but not so wide-ranging you run out of space to reach any interesting conclusions. Your tutors can help you narrow down a topic, once you have identified an area of interest. If you are having trouble fixing on an area you could think about what you have particularly enjoyed studying in your degree so far, what you wish you had had a chance to investigate further, or even look at the profiles of the staff in your department to see whether any of their research interests intrigue you. The important thing is to give time to choosing the right dissertation topic, which includes time to discuss options with tutors and friends, and investigate certain areas further by conducting your own library and internet research.

Points you should consider are:

- Will the topic hold your interest in the long term? It does not have to be related to a module you have taken or will be taking. This may be an opportunity to explore systematically an area of personal interest.

- In what way does the area you have chosen interest you?
- What *material* is available to help you answer these questions? Consult library catalogues, bibliographies of useful books found, reference materials, key databases for your subject. If in doubt, at this stage, ask tutors or library staff for guidance about where to look. How will you access the material you need? Will you need your tutor to help get you permission to access particular archives? Think about this now, because sometimes gaining access can take time.
- What useful skills can you learn or consolidate? Give some thought to the kind of experience you wish to gain and the skills you would like to acquire through the process of working on the dissertation. Clarifying your future plans may be relevant here.

If you have a particular career in mind, wish to continue to a higher degree or embark on further training, a carefully chosen dissertation topic could help to further your plans. You may wish to discuss these with a member of staff. We recommend an early visit to the Careers Service, where information on arts-related careers and funding as well as information on all types of careers is available. See **Chapter 7 – Life After University**.

The size and focus of the project

In order to get the scope of your project right – so that it is neither too large to cope with, nor too flimsy for proper academic discussion – you should avoid:

- Vague ideas – think through any idea as soon as possible by finding out more information about it to see if it will work.
- Hopeful suggestions – don't make any assumptions/suggestions which cannot be supported by research.
- Huge projects that will require a book to cover sufficiently – think about how the project could be split up into sections, and what you can realistically say in your word count (remember, you need to be accurate and detailed).
- Projects that do not build on taught areas – take advantage of the expertise you have developed so far.

The dissertation plan opposite provides a framework for the initial planning stage.

Dissertation Plan

TOPIC

Be as precise as possible about what you want to study and why. Make clear your reasoning, and detail factors such as the time period, geographical area, movements or particular people you will be looking at. Indicate your methodology – How will you be conducting your research? Will you be using a particular theoretical framework? What questions will you be asking of the material?

List the books, journals, articles and/or websites you have consulted so far. Also list any you intend to consult – and databases you have found useful in your initial search.

Indicate the source material you intend to use, and how you will access it.
Be as specific as possible.

List any tutor(s) you have consulted or would like to consult (if any)

EXAMPLE

A Contemporary Art Practice student wanted to do his dissertation on climate change. He had no previous experience of researching this topic and all the material he was finding about it was very scientific. He needed to find a way to connect it to an area he did know about – contemporary sculpture. Internet and library searches for 'climate change and contemporary sculpture' were too specific and did not help him find any useful information. However, he then began looking for information about art which dealt with environmental issues. This led him to a number of contemporary landscape and environmental artists – including Andy Goldsworthy – and through considering their work he came up with his topic – Environmental Art in the 21st Century: Three Case Studies.

Relationship with supervisor

You will be allocated a supervisor for your dissertation. This could be someone with a particular research interest in your topic, but it may not be. What you can guarantee, however, is that they will be an experienced researcher and well-qualified to advise on the scope, direction and structure of your project. It is often up to you to make the first contact with your supervisor and to request meetings with them; make sure you know how many supervisions you are entitled to have, and take advantage of the expertise they can offer. Your supervisor's role is as a research advisor; this means that, whilst they can recommend books for you to read, and research directions for you to go in, as well as discuss your ideas with you, they are not there to proofread your work, and will usually not be allowed to read a whole draft. It is important to establish how much they can read from the very beginning. If it is the case that they are willing to read drafts of chapters, work out how much notice they will need – this will obviously affect when you should be writing drafts.

How should a dissertation be structured?

A dissertation should involve testing out a hypothesis through research and discussion. This traditionally involves the following sections.

Abstract

This consists of a paragraph summary of the whole dissertation indicating your hypothesis, main argument, primary methodology, and main conclusions.

Introduction

The length of the introduction depends on the length of the project and whether the first chapter plays any kind of introductory role. A good guideline is for the main introduction to be 10% of the whole project. The introduction should draw the reader into your thinking behind the project. What is the purpose of the project? Why is it important to be researching what you are researching? What is the context for your research (who has researched similar topics – what conclusions did they come to?). Why is it interesting? What is your main argument? What conclusions do you come to? How is the project structured and why? Addressing these questions in the introduction is necessary to clarify for the reader the ultimate direction of your project.

Methodology section

Everyone researches according to some methodology – your methodology is simply how you have chosen to investigate your hypothesis. In scientific and social science subjects it often involves performing tests or undertaking surveys. In Arts and Humanities subjects, however, it is more likely to involve analysing written and/or visual data. For example, whilst an English literature dissertation may entail performing analyses of particular novels, comparing them, as well as comparing what others have said about them, a History dissertation could involve making an assessment of how a specific historical event has been represented by different historians, comparing their views to the evidence drawn from different primary sources. The importance of the methodology section is that it makes it clear to your reader how you are going to research and why. You may choose to look at a subject from a particular theoretical standpoint (for example, Feminism, or Marxism). This is also something you should discuss in the methodology section.

Results section

In a science or social sciences dissertation the results section is often separate, summarising the results – with no further comment – from the tests and surveys undertaken (as described in the methodology section). This often involves presenting information in tables, diagrams and graphs. In Arts and Humanities subjects, any results are more likely to develop from close readings of texts or visual media and analyses of different sources. As discussed further below, you *may not* have a separate results section because your analyses are likely to include discursive comment as well. If you *do* need to have a separate results section, it should involve close readings or analyses without further comment – saving your conclusions for the discussion section.

Discussion of the results

The discussion should make clear what is interesting and significant about what you have found. As well as looking at your results, it could be used to question your methodology – would you have got different results with a different methodology, can you now think of a better way you could have undertaken the project. The discussion should also put your results into the context of other people's. As indicated above, it may be that it is more appropriate to combine the results section with the discussion of the results.

Conclusion

The conclusion's most basic job is to sum up what your project was about and what you have found. However, you want to avoid it being a simple compilation of the other sections – it is your final chance to persuade your reader that your project is of value, and your findings are interesting. To this end, it is good to place your findings within a wider context as well as considering their implications. How does your argument fit with what others have said? What do your findings suggest need to be researched next? What recommendations could you now make on the basis of your findings?

NOTE

Some departments and institutions like the dissertation to be formally structured according to these sections – however, many don't require it to be presented with these particular headings, but the principles remain the same. For example, even though you might not be expected to write a distinct methodology section, you will need to state somewhere how you are going about researching what you are researching. Similarly, whilst you may not have distinct results and discussion sections, you will need to indicate what your findings have been and what conclusions you can draw from them.

You may, however, be allowed to structure your dissertation in your own way so that the methodology is contained in your introduction, the results discussed in chapters as you go along. Having said this, all dissertations, like all books, have some kind of introduction and conclusion. Check with your department for formatting and structuring conventions.

Conclusion: the advantages of undertaking a dissertation

A dissertation will show that the writer knows their subject, the key facts and different points of view in it – but it also advances a point of view resulting from original research. Remember that 'original' does not mean 'something that's never been done before' but rather 'something that you do for yourself'. So, a dissertation will involve a lot of research – your work will display accuracy and skill and a discussion of a subject. It means that your discussion will give evidence of critical analysis, that is, standing back from your subject and weighing up pros and cons. It means you will show that you understand that, amongst other things, aspects of particular theories or viewpoints are open to question.

- The dissertation will therefore allow you to undertake a project of particular interest to you.
- It will give you the opportunity to manage and complete a long piece of writing independently. Through writing a dissertation you will use and improve your critical, analytic, research and writing skills – these are skills to emphasise on your CV.
- Finally, the dissertation should give you the chance to get to know a tutor better and think about what you might want to do after your degree.

Further help

Dissertations are a challenge; if you are struggling, you are not alone. There is plenty of help available to you. Here are two websites we recommend:

1. The Dissertation Workshop website: www.dissertationworkshop.com
    This site is good for finding strategies for dealing with any worry or anxiety you may feel when trying to work on your dissertation.
2. University of Southampton dissertation worksheet: www.studyskills. soton.ac.uk/studyguides/Writing%20Your%20Dissertation.doc
    You can print out this document which gives comprehensive advice for researching and writing the dissertation.

Specific writing difficulties

I have tried, in this chapter, to address some of the main challenges you will face when undertaking written work at university. I hope I have also emphasised the great opportunity writing gives you to formulate your own ideas, and make your own mark on a subject. However, for some students writing can remain a source of anxiety, and always seem a struggle. This can be the case, in particular, if you have a specific learning difficulty such as dyslexia or dyspraxia. It can also seem an extra challenge if you are returning to learning after a long break. This last section of the chapter is designed to help you feel less alone and less panicky about the problems you might be experiencing. I hope I have identified some of the main problems you might have when beginning to write at university; it would be useful for you to read through the issues, and the suggested ways of tackling them I have provided. As these might not be enough, I also recommend places you can get extra help; all universities have support systems in place to help students deal with problems they might be having. I cannot stress the importance of accessing this help – the worse thing you can do is struggle on in silence. So, see how far this chapter can help – and talk to your tutor about how to receive extra support if you really are finding it difficult to produce the kind of writing expected of you.

● Getting started – severe procrastination

The problem

You find writing is difficult and, because you have many different tasks to undertake, you find that you avoid the actual writing stage of your work leaving it until the last minute and so not giving it the time it needs.

Suggested strategies
- Set yourself realistic targets. Think about what you can achieve each day and moderate your timetable accordingly.
- Tackle the writing in bite-sized chunks so you are never having to do too much at once. (For example, when you have an idea, or find something useful in your reading, write a paragraph about it there and then.)
- Find a study space that has little distraction and give yourself incentives (such as having a cup of tea with a friend, or going for a run) to stay there until you have written, say, 500 words, or a particular section of writing.
- Use other people to help you set targets – have breaks together.
- Talk to others about ways they motivate themselves to work.
- Sometimes, it is good to move around. One particular space – however ideal it seemed in the first place, can become associated with procrastination. For example, if you find you are getting distracted at home, go to the library with a pen and paper and try to get focused again.
- You may be procrastinating because the work you are doing seems an impossible challenge – if you have other, easier work to do, do this in between short bursts of the more difficult work. Don't give up on the

difficult work, but identify what you are having problems with so you can ask others for help. This could also help you split the work into more manageable tasks.

- If these strategies don't work, and your work is suffering, go and talk to someone; see the options listed at the end of this chapter.

● Understanding the question

The problem

You may find you have continual problems understanding what you are supposed to do for set assignments. There may be words used in the questions you don't understand, or it may be that you are just not sure what questions are really asking you to discuss, or what particular focus they require.

Suggested strategies

- The most important thing to do is to go and see your tutor. All tutors have office hours designated to see students; these times are there for you to go and discuss difficulties you might be having with the module. To make the best use of the time it is a good idea to consider what you think the assignment might require first of all and then have prepared questions to ask your tutor to see if you are on the right track.
- If for any reason you cannot see your tutor you should have a personal tutor who could help, as well as the university support services which should have a facility providing study skills support.
- Academic dictionaries, and our section in this chapter on what different essay words mean, could also be useful.
- If you are unsure about whether you are answering the question correctly – even after an initially comforting discussion with a tutor, ask if they will read a detailed plan to make sure you are on the right track. Most tutors will be happy to do this – just don't expect them to read full drafts of your work.

● Planning and structuring work

The problem

Many students find that although they are working hard on their course, enjoying learning and spending a lot of time writing assignments, they are not getting good marks because they are not very good at planning and structuring their work. You may find you have a lot of great ideas, but that it is difficult shaping them into a coherent argument.

Suggested strategies

Everybody needs to spend time to work out how they plan best. See earlier in this chapter for different ideas and thoughts about planning and drafting your work. The most important thing to remember is that you need to spend time developing your own strategy and this may change for different kinds of assignments (pp. 91–3). You may find planning software useful. For example, *Inspirations*® and *Mind Genius*® are particularly useful pieces of software designed to help you plan using different visual devices such as mindmapping and colour coding. The principle of these programmes is simple, and something you can follow without the use of a computer: university essays are expected to produce logical linear arguments, but we do not all naturally think in a logical, linear way.

Therefore, you need to develop strategies to work out all the different things you want to say in an essay, and then work out how to put all these into a linear argument. Writing them all down in a spider diagram, or on post-it notes you can move around when thinking, or even in lists which can be colour-coded can help – once the ideas are down on paper, you then need to think about your response to the question. This could be done by talking it through with a friend, by mapping out different orders of your ideas on paper, or by even saying aloud different versions of the argument to yourself. Once you have worked out your argument, you should be able to work out a plan. It could be helpful, when you are learning to structure your own work, to note down how others form *their* arguments – if you find a model which works.

● Expressing yourself clearly

One of the most difficult things to achieve when dealing with complex ideas at university, is how to express your own thoughts in an accessible way others will understand. It is also one of the most important. Many students find they can say what they want to say when speaking to other people, but find it difficult to then write these ideas down. This can be very frustrating. Although there is not room in this section, or this book, for a comprehensive lesson in grammar and punctuation, we list below some strategies for getting your ideas clear to yourself – which is the first step on the ladder to achieving good writing – and then we discuss some passages of unclear writing, to think about why they are unsuccessful and how they could be improved.

How can you come to a clear understanding of what you think?

Talking

Discuss your ideas with others – if you think better verbally take advantage of other students by telling them about your ideas.

Imaginative note-taking

If you find writing in continuous prose difficult, don't rely on that to think through your ideas, use a more visually friendly approach instead. Follow your thought process through using a flow chart, or go through your notes, like you might an article, and list on a separate piece of paper the ones you want to turn into an argument.

Listening and reading

Get ideas about how to express yourself by listening to others, and reading academic material.

Learning to write clearly

Think about these examples of unclear writing – they are here to show you that:

- Almost every student struggles with writing clearly when they first get to university. This does not mean they are unable to deal with complex ideas; it simply means they have not learnt how to express themselves clearly yet.
- There are some common pitfalls that it is useful to identify at this stage, so that you can start learning how to avoid them by using more effective writing strategies.

Example 1

To support her idea that what is and is not behaviourally normal is culturally determined she points to many examples of diverse moral attitudes such as homosexuality which has been morally frowned upon in present-day society but in Plato's *Republic* is presented as one of the major means to the 'Good Life'.

This is difficult to read because there are too many ideas stuffed into one sentence. The writer would make her ideas clearer if she just slowed down, or tried not to say so much. It could simply be a problem of punctuation – with a few well-placed commas or semicolons her ideas could be clarified. However, changing the word order could also help. To show what I mean I will first list the ideas in the sentence:

- The philosopher under discussion (and it would have been better to name her) believes that what is and is not behaviourally normal is culturally determined.
- She illustrates this belief by giving examples of moral attitudes.
- One of these examples is the diverse attitudes about homosexuality.
- Whilst some in present-day society believe homosexuality to be immoral, Plato's *Republic* presented it as one of the major means to the 'Good Life'.

The main issue for clarity is that the philosopher's argument, and the way she makes it through example, are all put into the same sentence. It is therefore confusing for the reader; they have to work hard to digest all these ideas in one sentence. It would be easier, then, if the ideas were split up into two sentences, or if the sentence was punctuated more effectively. Here are two alternatives which present the ideas more clearly:

Alternative 1

Philosopher X believes that culture determines what is considered 'normal'. She uses many examples of diverse moral attitudes to illustrate this point such as homosexuality. Whilst some believe homosexuality to be morally wrong today, arguing it is a modern day 'perversion', she points out that it was considered one of the major means to the 'Good Life' in Plato's *Republic*.

Alternative 2

To demonstrate her hypothesis that culture determines what is considered normal behaviour, Philosopher X draws upon many examples of diverse moral attitudes; one particularly striking illustration occurs in her discussion of homosexuality in which she points out that, whilst some consider it immoral in present day society, Plato's *Republic* argued that it played a primary role in achieving the 'Good Life'.

Example 2

Philosophers such as Baudelaire publicly denounced photography's artistic potential, whereas Roland Barthes (1915–80) may dislike art photography, the photography that imitates painting, yet still sees photography as an art. He mentions the 'noéme', the essence, the 'punctum', being the little something that a photograph has that makes it special, however, primarily, he sees photography as a proof of the past; a "has-been" snippet. His *Camera Lucida* (1980) is his last book, and his only one entirely based on photography, and one of the founding books on photography critique of our age. He is, however, far from being the only philosopher or academic to write of the semiotic impact of and on photography along with Rosalind Krauss and Walter Benjamin.

This piece of writing also suffers from confused word order, and sentences which are trying to do too much at once; it takes two or three readings to work out what the student is really trying to say. Take the first sentence; it makes clear that it will be contrasting Roland Barthes' attitude to photography as an art form to Baudelaire's. However, it then adds that Barthes disliked art photography (seemingly like Baudelaire), yet *did* see photography as an art. The writer needs to slow down and explain, as a complex distinction is being made: the argument is that photography that imitates painting is disapproved of by both writers, but whereas Baudelaire could not see the potential for any photography to be considered artistic, Barthes did think of photography as artistic. What is not made clear here is why he disapproved of photography which imitated painting. (It is also left unclear whether this is the photography Baudelaire denounced.) The implication is that the writer will then discuss how photography, for Barthes, *could* be considered an art; however, this never really happens. The *implication* is that it is an art because each photograph has that certain something which makes it special, but this is not clearly stated.

The second sentence, too, is confused. The writing moves from talking about the 'little something', to discussing Barthes' work on photography more generally – this is confusing, because it does not give us any more information about why Barthes might consider photography to be art. It is also a puzzling sentence in itself; it tells us three things about *Camera Lucida* in a seemingly random order – it is his last book, his only one entirely based on photography, and it is one of the founding books on photography critique. If these points need to be made, should they be in this order and at the expense of further outlining Barthes' argument? Finally, the last sentence is not well structured – and so does not really make sense. It needs words adding to really work, at the moment Rosalind Krauss and Walter Benjamin are just added on. To make sense it should read: He is, however, far from being the only philosopher to write of the semiotic impact of and on photography, Rosalind Krauss and Walter Benjamin being other notable critics.

Alternative

Philosophers such as Baudelaire publicly denounced the possibility for photography to have artistic potential. Roland Barthes, however, whilst having problems with the art photography that aims to imitate painting, still sees photography to be art. In his only book based entirely on photography, *Camera Lucida*, he understands the art of photography to be found in the 'noéme', the essence, the 'punctum'; in other words, he believes each photograph has that little something which makes it special. The importance of photography for Barthes, however, is the way it can represent the past becoming a "has-been snippet". **[This seems to be leading into another section.]**

It must be noted, that whilst *Camera Lucida* has become one of the founding books on photography critique of our age, he is far from being the only theorist to write of the semiotic impact of and on photography; Rosalind Krauss and Walter Benjamin are two other notable critics.

Example 3

The observation research documented attempts to provide some evidence of a kind of science to the 'act of drinking'. The mass-observation study suggests: "our observations show that the majority of pub-goers tend, when drinking in a group, to drink level; and very often there is not a quarter of an inch difference between the depths of the beer in the glasses of a group of drinkers."

The observations have reached a conclusion in the article that people who drink in groups drink at similar speeds allowing for a potentially interesting insight into how people drink. Simply observing this behaviour though does not justify that there is scientific reasoning behind how people drink their pints. Thus the method of observation may be a success as drinking patterns are explored, but the analysis is by no means concrete conclusive evidence.

This writing is really unclear: the short sentences and repetition make it even more difficult to read. The first sentence is fine, and the quotation is well introduced. However, the sentence after the quotation does not do very much; it tells us that a potentially interesting insight is reached, but could – with the same number of words – begin to suggest what that insight is. Instead, it just seems repetitive, not saying much more than the quotation itself. Equally, the next sentences make some kind of argument, but could be taken further, helping the reader understand exactly what the problem with the mass-observation study is. For example, is it fair to say the study is suggesting there is a scientific reasoning behind the way people drink, or is it not simply saying they seem to drink at similar speeds when together? Does the quotation really show evidence that drinking patterns are explored, or are they not simply observed? (Is that not the point of the critique?) And if the analysis does not work as concrete, conclusive evidence, what would? These questions could have been avoided with more precise word usage. Think about whether the suggested alternative helps make things clearer.

Alternative

The observation research documented attempted to provide evidence of a kind of science to the 'act of drinking'. The researchers suggest: "[their] observations show that the majority of pub-goers tend, when drinking in a group, to drink level; and very often there is not a quarter of an inch difference between the depths of the beer in the glasses of a group of drinkers."

They ask us to appreciate their observation that people in groups start to drink at similar speeds as a valuable, scientific contribution to the study of behaviour in pubs. However, whilst their study remains useful at the level of observation, it is not rigorous enough to be held up as concrete conclusive evidence of a science to group drinking behaviour.

Even with this alternative, it feels as though we need to know what we would need for something to be concrete conclusive evidence. It is also not made clear in the quotation that the mass-observation researchers were claiming scientific credentials.

Top tips for writing clearly

- Avoid long sentences which try to contain many ideas. When reading through your work make sure each sentence contains one main idea, and that the commas are helpful to the meaning.
- Try reading sentences out or using some software which can read them out to you, such as Texthelp®.
- Avoid very short sentences as these can often fragment ideas. Again, read your work out; sometimes these sentences can be joined together using a comma or semicolon.
- Think about the word order in a sentence, and the sentence order in a paragraph. Think about what you are saying first and why. What is the point in the sentence? Is it supporting what you have said before? Is it adding an extra point? If you are listing things in a sentence, is it clear why you are listing them, and why they are in that order? Are you just putting in information because you know it, or is it important that you give it at that point, alongside everything else?
- Always ask yourself – Have I made my main point clear? Why am I writing this? What am I hoping to say? If you lose track of the answers, go back to your plan. Or read through what you have written, think about what you want to say, make a new plan, and try to follow it.

In summary
Writing is vital, writing can be fun, but writing is hard. You will not be the only one having difficulties – find help as soon as possible if you are finding it all a bit much.

Sources of advice

University support services
- Personal tutors.
- Study skills advisors (some universities have their own Skills Centre, or Writing Labs – it is worth checking out what your university offers by looking on the website, asking your tutors, or asking at the library).
- Specialist Dyslexia/Dyspraxia support usually in a Disability Services department.
- Student Counselling Service – these often run group sessions for study skills issues, and individual counselling sessions can be useful for helping identify why you might be having particular problems with your writing.

Student Union

- 'Nightline'/telephone advice: most unions provide this facility which gives you the opportunity to discuss any issues you might be having with other students.
- Support groups: the more you can talk to others about writing issues, the less they should seem like unsolvable problems.

Library and bookshop

All university libraries will contain different study skills books which you might find it useful to browse. Books we particularly recommend about the writing process are:

- *Writing at University* by Phyllis Creme and Mary R. Lea (Maidenhead: Open University Press, 1997)
  This guide will help you develop your planning processes in particular.
- *Studying English Literature* by Tory Young (Cambridge: Cambridge University Press, 2008)
  Like our guide, this book provides examples from students' work which should help you think about what tutors expect from work, as well as thinking about how to achieve it.
- *The Student's Guide to Writing* by John Peck and Martin Coyle (Basingstoke: Palgrave, 1999)
  This book goes into the detail we cannot about how to structure sentences effectively and use punctuation and grammar correctly, to make your writing clear.

Internet

There are some really helpful websites dealing with various writing issues. You need to be aware that many are aimed at students in the United States and Canada and some of their rules of grammar and punctuation are different. However, many websites are useful and have interactive exercises so you can test yourself. Websites we consider particularly useful are:

- 'Improving your Writing' by University of Bristol http://www.bristol.ac.uk/arts/exercises/grammar/grammar_tutorial/index.htm [Accessed 26.05.2009]
  Contains interactive exercises to help you learn how to use punctuation and grammar effectively.

- 'DISSC Live' by University of Teesside http://dissc.tees.ac.uk/mainmenu.html [Accessed 26.05.2009]
  Provides many examples from students' and published work to enable you to consider what effective writing involves.
- 'Essay Guide' by Dr. David Kennedy http://www.rlf.org.uk/fellowshipscheme/writing/essayguide.cfm [Accessed 26.05.2009]
  This guide is easy to use and accessible, written from the point of view of an Arts lecturer, thinking through how you can begin to meet the expectations of your tutors.

Summary

Written assignments will form the crux of your assessment at university; writing, moreover, will be one of your most important transferable skills when you move on to a career. As such, we have emphasised the need for you to think about how to plan and draft your writing, how to structure your work, and how to express your ideas in the most clear and precise way. Remember: a degree is not just about learning, and it does not only involve having ideas; it is about how those ideas are expressed. Learning to write is a continual process. Put time and thought into considering how you present your ideas, and how you put them into the context of a wider debate, and you will find you will begin to enjoy writing, and your tutors will enjoy your essays too.

6 Preparing For and Taking Examinations

● Introduction

This chapter aims to help you prepare for and take examinations; it provides ideas about how to develop your own revision techniques and manage your time effectively. For most Arts and Humanities subjects you will be required to write essays in exams and so, rather than rote-learning information to regurgitate, you need to be able to think critically about the course material and answer the exam questions in a discursive and analytical way.

Before we start thinking about good revision strategies, let's think about what makes for good examination results. In other words, what are you aiming to achieve? What do you need to produce in an exam? A group of Arts and Humanities lecturers at the University of Leeds came up with the following list of features most often found in high-scoring examination papers.

Students who do well in exams:
(a) answer the question set by the examiner
(b) demonstrate detailed knowledge and apply it to the question
(c) structure their answers effectively around a clear argument: this means selecting judiciously from what you have revised rather than including everything that you know
(d) demonstrate a clear understanding of the broader conceptual issues of the module
(e) write fluently and clearly
(f) often show good awareness of scholarly literature and debates surrounding the module content

All of these features of good exam responses require students to demonstrate both familiarity with the course material, and an ability to apply their knowledge to the construction of relevant, convincing and coherent arguments. In other words, successful students do not simply repeat chunks of information; rather, they convert the material they have learnt into responsive, thoughtful discussions. To get to this point, they will have actively engaged with the material before the examination. This chapter will show you some ways to revise actively, and so get to a point where you can apply your knowledge effectively.

What does successful revision involve?

Most importantly, effective revision requires taking an approach to your subject which is less utilitarian and more engaged. This means you must develop a certain mindset which guards against seeing revision as just the storage of information in your short-term memory. You must remember some pertinent information, of course, but examinations in the Arts and Humanities are not designed to see how well you can learn by rote. This makes sense if you think about why you are studying in the first place: when you chose your degree subject and modules, it was not simply to prove you could memorise material. It was to get to know and have an opinion about areas of interest and perhaps to develop an understanding about topics key to a potential career of choice. Throughout the semester and within the revision period, you will need to think about the material with an investigative interest, rather than as a means to an end – this end being a mark and a qualification. The attitude I am advocating involves thinking of your revision in three key ways.

1. Active

You need always to be doing something with the material you are revising. You need to be thinking about why you are learning it, and how to apply your knowledge in different, relevant situations.

2. Cumulative

Because you are revising, you have seen the material before – it makes sense, then, to make sure when you are first learning the material to acknowledge you will always be building upon what you learn. The lectures and small group discussions you will attend throughout the semester are ultimately part of your revision process. Each will contribute to your understanding of the module.

3. An individual and collaborative process

In an examination you will need to show a critical awareness of the subject – this means acknowledging the ideas of others but also showing you have your own ideas about a topic. To do this, when revising, and throughout the module, you need to keep track of your response to the ideas of others. It also means that in the revision period you might not simply be revisiting these ideas, but you may well also be undertaking more research in the library to build up a resource of background knowledge, and so develop your own critical stance further.

● Active revision: keeping your mind alert

One of the most important things to remember when beginning to revise is that you will learn more effectively if you keep your brain stimulated by doing something with the information beyond simple rote learning. Most examinations for Arts and Humanities subjects require you to write discursive essays and so you will need to demonstrate that you not only have a grasp of the subject, but that you have developed your own assessment of it, and can use your knowledge of it and ideas about it to produce a relevant response to the question. In other words, ideally, you will need to show that you can think independently, and that you have both an overview of a subject and knowledge of the details. This will help you illustrate any argument you produce with examples relevant to the question.

To achieve this level of understanding, and to develop your own critical voice in relation to the subject, you need to find a way to continue to engage with the material as you have been doing throughout the semester. Many make the mistake of planning to simply re-read set texts and notes – this is a pretty inefficient and ineffectual way of learning the material because your relationship with it remains passive. As discussed in the **Reading Strategies** chapter, you can develop a complex understanding of your revision material much more easily if you ask inquiring questions of it and investigate it with a purpose beyond 'learning' it off by heart.

Below are some ideas for making your revision active. They all involve the process of questioning yourself and your revision material to keep your mind active and focused on what you need to learn and why. The more you test yourself in your revision, the easier being tested in the examination

---

TIP
Revision is best done on a regular basis. This will help you get the information into your long-term memory. Moreover, it stands to reason that if you only revise some material once, and in one way, then there is more chance it will only stay in your short-term memory, and might not be so easy to recall in the exam. However, if you revise material in different ways and get used to recalling it to illustrate different arguments, it should become an established part of your long-term memory to be drawn upon when needed.

should become. The idea is that you will become familiar enough with the material from a module as a whole that you could:

- have a complex discussion about it;
- understand the arguments from different points of view;
- be able to put issues into a wider context.

Six active revision strategies

1. **Test yourself** by thinking of a concept and writing down all you know about it. Check your answer and identify areas you missed or realise that you don't fully understand. You will need to revise these areas.
2. **Revise with others**. Studying with others, e.g. in study groups, brings other people's ideas and understanding to the table. This allows you to exchange, clarify and expand your own understanding of the subject.
3. **Re-organise your notes**. Look back over all your notes for common themes/ideas etc. Link these together to develop your understanding of that topic.
4. **Use visual aids**. Draw maps, diagrams, flow charts, pictures etc, to see and create associations. These are generally easier to remember than 'slabs of text'. Use highlighter pens.
5. **Use past exam papers**. Look at past exam papers and practise answering them. Practising past exam questions helps you to prepare for and predict the sort of questions that might be asked and to work out the best possible answers. Create mock questions and bullet point your answers. This is more effective than trying to learn by rote.
6. **Review your course work**. Look for strengths and weaknesses in your understanding. Fill in these gaps. Review lecturers' comments from lectures or from your assignments.

More thoughts on using past papers

One of the strategies suggested above is to use past exam papers. These are usually made available through the university library, or Virtual Learning Environment. Ask your tutor and/or library staff if you have trouble accessing them. For some modules there may be no past papers available – it may be that it is the first time the module has run, for example. In this case it is worth asking the tutor whether they can provide some practice questions or topics. If you have been given a choice of essay questions throughout the semester this could be used for practice; at this stage you could also work with fellow students to think up practice questions as suggested above. This process can really help you think about what the module's aims have been, and so, approach your revision in a self-conscious, reflective and investigative manner.

Use past papers to:

- Identify areas of revision – and to get an idea of how questions will be asked. This could help you practice answering the question – see the section **Answering the question** (p. 155) for further thoughts on this.
- Practise your own exam technique by doing a timed mock exam. This could be useful for identifying holes in your knowledge early in your revision schedule and so help you focus on what you need to revise more thoroughly.
- Revise with friends, choosing a question and then discussing how you would answer it (perhaps each drawing up a plan individually under timed conditions to then compare afterwards).

Memory techniques

For some exams you will need to memorise some information, whether it is the names and dates of certain authors, philosophers, texts or historical events, grammar rules, the phonetic alphabet or a passage from critical material that you might quote in the exam. There are techniques to help you remember information – and whole books out there detailing ways to improve your memory. However, some particularly common, effective methods are listed below.

Effective memory strategies

Monitor your comprehension

You can only remember and fully utilise ideas that you understand. Find ways to monitor your comprehension. Get in the habit of saying to yourself, "Do I understand this?" Always check the logic behind the ideas – do things happen in a way that you would predict? If you can see the logic in something, you are much more likely to be able to reconstruct that idea even if you cannot immediately recall it. Also, look out for anything that seems counter-intuitive to you: you are less likely to remember something that does not seem logical or something that you would not agree with. Evaluate your own comprehension by bouncing your thoughts about key module issues against those of other students. One really effective strategy for checking how much of a grasp you have of a subject is to tutor another student who is having difficulty; if you teach someone else, you reinforce your own knowledge and find out, if you cannot explain things so well, where you may need to revise further.

Generate your own examples

Go beyond examples provided in class and in the text, and bring your general knowledge and experiences into play by relating them to academic ideas. When you can generate your own examples, you demonstrate your understanding, and your memory is enhanced.

Use your senses – become aware of what triggers your memory

Concrete images are more memorable than abstract ideas; visual aids can really help you learn. It can be useful, then, to begin consciously associating your own mental pictures with the academic content. Use colour to highlight headings and other key ideas in your notes. Use shapes to help you organise ideas; triangles, boxes, flow charts, circles. Some people think spatially, so it could also be useful to use your room as a memory aid – certain pieces of information can be posted on the wall above the desk, others by the bed, others above the mirror. Then when you recall, you can remember where they were in the room. The key is to think about what helps you remember – for some people, colour really triggers memories, other people remember where something was on the page, and others remember where they were when they had a conversation about a topic. Once you have established what helps you remember the most effectively, begin to formulate a revision strategy around this. For example, if talking about a subject helps you articulate what you know, perhaps you could record your ideas, as well as talk to others. Further, more than one strategy can help. A student of mine would begin with colour-coding her lecture notes, she would then make up similarly colour-coded index cards with a question on one side and an answer summary on the other. This meant she could get people to test her who did not have to be specialists in the subject. Then she worked from past papers – producing flow charts of how she would respond, initially referring to the colour-coded cards when necessary. This layering of revision strategies really helped her consolidate her understanding of the subject, the different reorganisations of the information meant that she was always doing something with the information, learning it through categorising it, summarising it, discussing it and using it to respond to past papers.

The following example shows the kind of process this student went through.

Colour-coding lecture notes

I am using the example from Chapter 2. See page 36 for the lecture notes before they were colour-coded – shown as shading in this book.

24/10/09
French autobiography Lecture 1

<u>Why are writers drawn to autobiography?</u>

- To achieve sthg; to learn sthg about self (La Bâtarde)
- To achieve understanding, absolution, forgiveness from reader
- To instruct or impress the reader (Sartre, Gide, Beauvoir)
- To elicit form of love from reader (Leduc)
- To ward off effect of aging (Beauvoir)

> Why write – authors are attracted to autobiography

Authors have diff. emotional involvement in autob. than fiction.

More complex reasons

- Lack. Freud and Lacan have suggested that human subject has no core single entity with an 'essence' or 'wholeness'
  ⇨ autob. allows writer to define self, give self shape. Autob., then, is v. reassuring (not to describe ourselves but to <u>construct</u> a self) → see 'Qui est-ce ce Violette Leduc?' See quote 3 handout 1.
  We have a gap and writing makes us whole.
  One stage further, see quote 4, we see life as chaotic and arbitrary and Autob. gives it shape and direction. → Autob. as THERAPY. driven by a "will to form" (M. Sheringham), to make life ordered + meaningful. Impose order of present on chaos of past.

> Lack and psychoanalysis – as reason for autobiography

- Duty. Feeling of having to constitute moral lesson about being → often set self up as negative example (Sartre, Sachs – Beauvoir sets self up as positive but for same reason)

> Duty and morality – as reason for autobiography

- To write the 'great work'. For people who've already reached the pinnacle of career, this is a final gesture. Should be well-known B4 writing Autob.

> To write great work – as reason for autobiography

Expected traits of autobiography as a genre

<u>What does the genre claim to achieve?</u> (classic autoB.)
– It's a referential narrative form (relates to the real): the 1st message we receive is that <u>reality</u> of the past life is captured in the text.
– It's telling the 'truth' about its subject
– The story it offers is a sincere story.

These 3 messages are v. problematic + flawed because:
– The autoB. will always be selective (Beauvoir attempts to mask this but necessarily fails)
– An author can't know the truth about himself. Aspects of his past won't be transparent to him.
– When author chooses to write a self-portrait, the facts will be chosen to create a particular self-image (Beauvoir, Sartre)

Why auto will always be flawed

Subject bent on freedom   subject living in bad faith

****So Autob. will always be PARTIAL, in both senses of the word.
Subject of AutoB. narrative will never coincide completely with the writing subject, ref quote 5: the present author bears on conception of younger subject: the author wants to be seen in a certain way: both a referential, real subject, and a narrative creation.

PLUS, language cannot tell the truth. Quote 6. Words have a tangential relation to the real. Language evolves, meaning changes with time. As autoB. is a linguistic artefact, it cannot be true.
BUT, if autoB. doesn't tell THE truth, it does tell A truth. Not objective, not total – it's partial + biased but is nonetheless a truth that the author wants to embrace. At the least, autoB. tells us sthg about autobiographer at time of writing.
Most authors DO NOT claim to offer the whole truth.

Making up index cards

Put the question on one side and the main answers on the other. Examples of a couple are:

> Why are authors attracted to auto?
> - To achieve sthg; to learn sthg about self (La Bâtarde)
> - To achieve understanding, absolution, forgiveness from reader
> - To instruct or impress the reader (Sartre, Gide, Beauvoir)
> - To elicit form of love from reader (Leduc)
> - To ward off effect of aging (Beauvoir)

> Examples of writing auto to learn sthg about self.
>
> Violette Leduc's <u>La Bâtarde</u>
> Helped Leduc realise:
> – how she was affected by her mother's hostility
> – as a child she suffered from a negative self-image – e.g.
>   [example quote would be good here]
> – how influential relationship with grandmother was
>
> ***this book also goes beyond the self making useful comments on female identity and social conditions
> ***not just therapeutic – literary

Working from past papers

I will use the example question: 'For Twentieth Century French Writers, autobiography always provides the opportunity, not to simply to narrate a life story, but to construct a self.' Discuss.

> **Plan 1**
> Is it possible to narrate life story? Need to think about what autoB aims to do:
> - It's a referential narrative form (relates to the real): the 1st message we receive is that reality of the past life is captured in the text.
> - It's telling the 'truth' about its subject
> - The story it offers is a sincere story.

So – auto aims to be real, true and sincere. →
This is one of the reasons writers are attracted to it as it would
help them learn something about themselves – e.g. Leduc's La
Bâtarde and Beauvoir's Memoirs of a Dutiful Daughter
What examples do I have of them learning?
⇨
BUT this moves beyond agenda of truth telling because:
  • Also used as a way to explore lack and construct more positive
    version of self – talk about FREUD and LACAN
  • Works as a confession – wants absolution from reader e.g.?
  • Stories work as a teleological narrative (narrative with a clear
    progressive design) containing moral lessons e.g.?

Argument and Conclusion: It is actually impossible for any auto to
just tell story of a life, but ALSO author cannot control self they
construct – Leduc and Beauvoir both read by feminists as talking
about issues beyond themselves
They create themselves as literary characters who can be
interpreted in different ways
BUT we still somehow read autoB differently – still some
connection to the truth?

I hope this student's example has shown you the different ways you can
make your notes work for you – and how they can be turned into interactive
revision tests and ultimately form part of your own argument in essays and
exams.

Use mnemonics

Mnemonics are memory training devices or ways of making associations to
aid in remembering. They can be extremely powerful; at the same time, if
you overuse mnemonics, you can spend too much time on generating and
learning the mnemonics and too little time on real understanding of the
material. However, the economical use of mnemonics to study for a test can
be very effective.

Mnemonics can be constructed in several ways:

●   Rhymes can be powerful; psychology students, for example might
     begin to remember Freud's personality theory in the little rhyme, "Id
     is the kid!"

- Acronyms collapse the beginning letters of a set of information into one or a few words; in trigonometry, you can use SOHCAHTOA for right-angled triangles; in French you can use DR and MRS VANDER-TRAMPP for verbs that conjugate with être.
- The beginning letters of a set of information can be built into a sentence; All Cows Eat Grass and Every Good Bird Does Fly are mnemonics used by people learning to read music.

These are just a few of the many types of mnemonics that you can use. As you study for your tests, use your imagination to generate fitting mnemonics for some of the key information in your courses.

Repetition

The more times you go over something, the better your memory will be of that information. However, each time you go through something, try to find a different angle so that you are not just repeating exactly the same activity. By varying your approach, you will create more connections in long-term memory.

Organising and coding your notes

Finally, with revision you will have sets of notes from different sources: lectures, seminars, reading. It can help to spend some time putting these in order, color-coding them, and adding to them throughout the revision period. Going through what you have can act as a reminder of what you have learnt, it can be the beginning of the process of re-visiting and re-using information, and could be useful in highlighting what more you need to learn. Keeping all the notes for one topic together will obviously save you time when you come to revise that topic, and can be quite a comforting way for you to realise that you have actually learnt quite a lot about the subject throughout the semester.

● Cumulative revision: a culmination of your learning throughout the semester

How do lectures and group discussions help you pass exams?

All university teaching in one way or another is designed to help you pass your exams. With exams, tutors aim to test how much you have engaged with the module as a whole – as well as to find out what information you know. In other words, exams assess what you can do with the information you have learnt. This means it is helpful to think of lectures and group discussion classes as key resources for your revision: they provide the stepping stones for your learning, each taking you closer to the stage you need to be at when sitting the exam. As well as imparting valuable information, your lecturers give you the opportunity to improve your critical thinking, by presenting well-constructed, and often provocative arguments in the lecture to compare to your own take on the subject; further they give you a chance to discuss the issues and test your own ideas with a group. By thinking of lectures and group discussions as part of your revision process, you will be acknowledging that preparation for your exams begins from the outset of any module; this means it is imperative that you become actively involved with what is happening in lectures and discussions from the start (and this means preparing for both by reading set texts and supplementary material). The notes you take throughout the semester will become crucial at the revision stage – really helping you get a critical grasp on the subject.

Lectures

Lectures are designed as a starting point to your own critical thinking. Sometimes they provide an insight into the wider context of your area of study; sometimes they provide an example of a particular argument in the field; sometimes they offer you indicative ways of reading or approaching a specific text, issue or event. Consequently, your lecture notes should work as a starting point for your revision – but they should not be the only thing you revise. Use them to get a handle on the areas you need to revise in more depth then go to the library and read books and journal articles to develop your knowledge of the subject.

Classes and group discussions

Classes and group discussions help you think through the main concepts on the course with other people; they give you a context to discuss the ideas raised in lectures and secondary reading and to give you some guidance on further independent research you need to pursue. They also give you an opportunity to talk to tutors about what you need to revise. (You can also go to see tutors on a one-to-one basis in their consultation hour.) Just as lectures are designed as a starting point to your own critical thinking, university classes give you the chance to respond critically to ideas through discussion with others. Use this opportunity wisely by taking an active part in the discussion whilst in class and writing up the most important parts of the discussion later to remind yourself of areas you would like to pursue and revise in more depth.

Revision as an individual and collaborative process

Revision is a process of continual learning. This process is potentially infinite. I do not say this to make it seem an impossible task, but to help you see it is not one which can be finished comprehensively – a subject can never be learnt, only understood in increasingly complex ways. Similarly, if you only try to re-learn lecture notes you will limit your scope for an original response in an exam. However, if you think of revision as an ongoing process, then you can use your revision time to continue learning and thinking about the subject and so enter the exam with fresh, new ideas, being in the zone of thinking about the subject, not hoping to end thinking about it. Revision is not simply a reminder of old ideas – it is a process in which you should be continually developing and getting to grips with new ones.

Making good use of the library during revision time

In summary, then, exams are your opportunity to demonstrate not only what you know about a subject, but how you can think critically and analytically about it. This means that the library – which provides a wealth of resources – is your revision friend: you can use it to find the material from the reading lists and beyond; the more perspectives you can get on a subject, and the more material you find to bounce ideas off, the more your critical opinion on a subject can be honed to a sophistication you can demonstrate in the exam. In other words, do not rely on your notes from lectures and small group teaching material in the exam, heighten your critical approach and knowledge of the subject by engaging with additional contextual and critical material. When you are going through your lecture and seminar notes at the beginning of the revision period:

- identify what you feel you could know more about;
- note down any areas of interest you would enjoy researching further;
- highlight for yourself any recommended further reading which you did not investigate at the time.

These three tasks will help you decide what to research in the library. Reading new material, and noting down your response to it should keep you interested and stimulated during the revision period as well as give you a more varied idea of a topic and so a more diverse personal response to it. Use the **Reading** and **Research** sections of this book for further ideas and information about how to find revision material.

> **Tip**
> Whilst I recommend that you keep revision stimulating by researching mate-
> rial, there needs always to be a cut-off point, when you stop researching
> and start consolidating what you know. Making a timetable which incor-
> porates each stage of the revision process is, therefore, a good strategy.
> After all, you will usually have more than one exam to do, and the revision
> period will not be infinite.

The library is also a place you can meet other people and confer with them to see if you can help each other revise and share resources. Don't forget, if you are easily distracted, to find your own corner in which to hide and concentrate. Libraries also contain useful reference books for each subject that can help you confirm precise facts and figures to help with the exam. For example, if revising for an Art History exam, reading about Modernism and focusing upon Cubism, you might find yourself identifying George Braques as essential but be unfamiliar with what his work actually looks like, whilst not being sure of when he was painting, exactly. An encyclopaedia about Art and Artists could give you the quick summary you need to see if you should investigate further. Encyclopaedias and dictionaries can really help you fill in the gaps and give you a more precise picture, as long as you back up this basic knowledge with more complicated critical reading.

Organising and managing your revision time

The revision period can be a stressful time. From having structured teaching time, you are thrown into a situation in which you have a bulk of time you need to structure yourself. The key thing, then, is to actually *structure* it! Otherwise, it is easy to fritter, procrastinate, faff and worry the time you *do* have away. We would therefore strongly advise making some kind of timetable. You may well have come to this conclusion yourself – I don't think there is any harm, however, in thinking through how to make a useful and realistic exam timetable:

- Always begin with listing everything that you will need to revise for in the exam period.
- When considering which subjects need revising, split them up into smaller topics to help break up your revision into more manageable, bite-sized pieces.

- Once you have a list of topics, decide when you will revise and what, taking into consideration the date of the exam, of course.
- Factor time into your revision timetable to organise your notes – this will help you work out any gaps you have in your knowledge.
- Make time to collaborate with friends, as well as time for reading in the library, and learning independently.
- Some people work better by varying their environment, others can concentrate more easily in the same focused space. Think about which kind of person you are and arrange your timetable accordingly.
- Life does not usually stop during exam time. Also, it can be useful to give your brain a break and do other activities – this can even make the time you have dedicated to revision more efficient. Therefore, factor into your timetable positive, non-revision time. Particularly productive activities involve exercise – anything you find fun, even a brisk walk can help – which gets the endorphins to the brain, helping freshen and re-stimulate the mind. Anything you find relaxing and therapeutic like cooking, tidying or playing music can also help reserve your intellectual energy for the next revision stint. Watching television for long periods is not such a good activity, however. The amount of visual and aural stimulation is not relaxing and can just switch your brain into a kind of mush-like state rather than truly relaxing it. However, short bursts of a favourite programme would not hurt. Focused coffee breaks with friends can help – but not if they involve large caffeine intakes and panicked conversations about how much everyone has to do. Drinking water and distracting yourself with a completely stress-free topic of conversation is the way forward, although difficult advice to take.
- Make a realistic timetable you will follow. There is no point in making a timetable which seems impossible and intimidating. Your brain cannot really focus properly for more than about eight hours a day. Timetable for this amount, varying your activities to get the most out of the day and feel as though you have achieved useful objectives.
- Finally, think about when you usually do your most productive work. Some people work best in the morning, others in the afternoon or evening. Timetable in the work you will need to concentrate the most on in these periods – for example, reading or memorising – using other times of the day to do less intensive work like colour-coding, finding material in the library, or revising with others.

Look at the example of Mark who is taking History and Theology and has four exams, listed in the order he has to take them:

Russian Revolution: worth 10 credits
Philosophy of Religion: worth 20 credits
African Religion: worth 10 credits
Canada and Multiculturalism: worth 15 credits

Figure 6.1 (pp. 152–3) shows a timetable for his last week of revision.

This student has factored in time for rest and exercise; tried to vary the kind of study activities he is doing; prioritised the subject he will be examined on first and also the one worth more marks – whilst trying not to neglect the others; decided where he is going to be studying; and allowed left some blank slots to allow for flexibility. Think about this timetable; do you think it would work? Remember that he will have done revision before; this is here as an example of *one* way to organize your time and study multiple subjects, the week before your exams start.

● Non-essay exams – some guidelines

You won't always be expected to write conventional essays in exams – these are the most challenging and the most prevalent, which is why we have focused most of this chapter on them. However, there are other forms of examination in Arts and Humanities degrees. Below I give guidelines to the most common.

Short-answer questions – or gobbets

These ask for succinct responses, designed for you to demonstrate what you have learnt in a couple of sentences or a paragraph.

Suggested strategies for answering short-answer questions

1. Don't spend too long on each answer.
2. Try to organise your ideas logically and present a coherent response.
3. Think what points, key words, ideas or phrases the examiner may be looking for.
4. Answer the questions given. Do not just write about the topic.
5. Leave one or two lines after each answer in case you remember something important later on.

Oral exams

These are mainly restricted to language modules in which they are usually testing your command of the language and sometimes of the subject as well. As with other exams, it is important that you respond to the questions being asked. You should be given the opportunity to speak the language in discussions – the more you do this and find native speakers to talk with, the more confident you will be in an oral exam. There is not the room to go into more details about this here – your department and tutors should give you support for this kind of exam. You may also want to see what support your university skills centre provides about doing well in oral presentations.

Analysing unseen passages

To test your reading skills, some exams may contain an unseen passage from a poem, play, novel, historical source or philosophical text. You will have to provide an analysis of it, usually putting into the context of the module's concerns as a whole. Advice about how to read critically in Chapter 3 should help you with this (p. 57). If you know you are going to have to do this kind of exam, practise it beforehand by picking random passages and seeing what kind of analysis you can come up with. Pay particular attention to: the choice of words, the structure of the passage, whether you can identify where it comes from and what it could be compared to. This kind of question requires you to see how you can apply the knowledge you have learnt to an analysis of an unprepared piece, so it is most important to remember to:

- Read the piece carefully.
- Plan a structured, coherent response which involves critical thinking.
- Think about how to bring in the context of the module as a whole.

The exam itself

If you have revised the material in a thoughtful and engaged way – doing something with it, rather than just simply trying to memorise it, then the exam should take care of itself: that's the ideal situation, anyway. However, it is good to work on your examination technique, as it can be very different trying to recall and utilise information in pressurised timed conditions, than it is in the comfort of your own home. The essence of good exam technique involves four things.

	Monday	Tuesday	Wednesday
Morning 9–1	**Phil of rel** – working with lecture and reading notes – identifying themes from past papers and syllabus	[9–11] <u>at home</u> **Russian revolution**: Revise one area using reading and lecture notes to produce a flow chart of events. [11–1] swimming	[9–11] **Russian Revolution**: discuss how to answer past paper and made up questions with friend [11–1] read article to improve critical understanding of a specific area
1–2		L	U
Afternoon 2–6	**Phil of rel** – reading articles to fill in knowledge gaps	<u>In library</u>: revise 2nd area for **Russian Revolution**, producing another flow chart – filling in knowledge gaps if necessary	<u>In library</u>: revisit **African Religion** notes, identifying areas which need further investigation – Find and begin reading 2 articles
	Walk home from uni to clear head	B Meet friend to discuss **Russian Revolution** & eat	R
Evening 8–11	**Phil of Rel** Think about past papers and new reading – begin planning arguments	1 hr revise **Russian Revolution** facts 1 hr make up own exam questions to ask friend	

Figure 6.1   Sample revision timetable

Thursday	Friday	Saturday	Sunday
Revisit **Phil of Rel.** What don't I understand? Use texts books and articles to ensure understanding What problems issues do I have with the ideas of others? – make a spider diagram making clear thoughts of others, and how I fit in.	<u>At home:</u> Revisit **Canada** notes, and think about them using a map and timeline Use text book to fill in any knowledge gaps	<u>Home</u> – [10-12] – revisit **Phil of Rel** notes to prepare for: [12-1] write essay in timed conditions	FINAL DAY FOR **RUSSIAN REVO** [9-11] REVISIT NOTES IN PREP FOR: [11-1] – MOCK EXAM – WRITE PAST PAPER WITH NO NOTES
N Meet friend	*C* Walk to library	*H*	
[2-4] Write essay plans from past papers for **African Religion** Read through essay plans and discuss with friend – do they make sense? What have I not thought of?	[2-6] revise 4 different writings about **multiculturalism** What are the problems and benefits of each?	[2-4] think about essay – what could have been added? What do I need to brush up on? [4-6] extra **phil of rel** reading	Analyse mock exam answers, use notes and articles to expand thinking on what is written – transfer any hard-to-remember names, dates etc ... onto index cards
E	*A*	*K*	
	Reward myself by going out for a drink to relax – BUT – need to work tomorrow so not too much. Home by midnight.		Use index cards to revise final facts etc... Get an early night (bed by 10:30) Read something unrelated to help sleep.

1. Making sure you know exactly what is expected of you in the exam

Consulting past papers should help with this, as well as making sure you have clearly understood the course information you should receive from your tutor. If you are unclear about anything – ask your tutor. Exams can be given in different formats, so it is good to become really familiar with what you are going to have to do in each module. This could involve – as suggested in the past papers section – actually practising the exam in timed conditions. It could also involve discussing the format and expectations with other students and the staff. It is also a good idea to look at the marking criteria, which can usually be found in module and departmental handbooks.

2. Managing your time so you can address all parts of the exam

Good time management in the exam is crucial – the worst thing is to run out of time before you have reached your really crucial points. The easiest way to lose marks is to spend a lot of time on one question and run out of time to finish the others. If you have an exam which consists of two essays with equal weighting, for example, there are only so many marks you can get per question. It is not a good use of your time to spend the majority on one question at the expense of the other, even if you are more confident in answering the first. Each essay will still count as 50% of your final mark, so the unfinished one could really bring the whole mark down. The best thing to do is to decide a time strategy before you go in. It could look something like this:

Exam: 2 hours long. 2 essays – each worth 50%
First 10 mins: choosing the questions.
Next 10 mins: planning answer for first essay. Next 35 mins writing the essay.
Next 10 mins: planning answer for the second essay.
Next 35 mins: writing the essay.
Final 20 mins: reading over answers, making any additions which would make the arguments clearer and more persuasive and knowledgable.

You will notice that in this plan I have factored in a lot of planning and editing time. This will be needed if you are going to be writing essays – as you will be partly judged on your ability to construct a thoughtful, convincing argument in response to the question. You need time, therefore, to think through this argument – and to make any additions once you have the bulk of it down. Obviously, this is just a suggested plan. Suffice to say, you should think about your timing plan before you enter the exam room. That way, you walk in prepared and hopefully can just execute the plan!

3. Responding to *and* answering the questions

There cannot be enough emphasis put on the importance of this point. You need to answer the question you are asked – not the ones you want to be asked! You can practise applying your knowledge to exam questions by consulting past papers. It is also something you will have practised in your written assignments – see Chapter 4 (p. 70) for advice on what essay questions are asking for.

> It is essential that you give yourself planning time in an exam so that you can read through the questions carefully, think about what they are asking, and plan your responses accordingly. Don't just start writing in a panic!

The ability to answer the question is fundamental to the writing of an effective exam answer. By looking at past papers you can often identify the kinds of themes and issues which are going to come up on your paper, but it is not enough to identify the general theme and then write all you know about it. You need to organise your answer so it is responding directly to the question as it is asked.

EXERCISE **Answering the question**

Consider these two sets of examples which demonstrate how questions which address the same theme can come from different perspectives. Each requires an individual response which addresses the particular areas upon which the question is focused.

English Literature past exam questions – general theme: the representation of gender in *Wide Sargasso Sea* and *Jane Eyre*
Each of the three questions below asks the student to think about how gender is represented in the two novels and follows a similar format: the student is asked to discuss a quotation. These quotations are very different, however, and a successful exam answer will explore the implications of the quotation in depth within a discussion of the two novels. Think about the essay questions as part of the exercise.

a. "[A] man's sentence ... was a sentence that was unsuited for a woman's use" (Virginia Woolf). Discuss the relationship between language and gender in *Jane Eyre* and *Wide Sargasso Sea*.

Exercise continued

b. 'In feminist terms, the representation of gender in *Wide Sargasso Sea* does not represent an advance, but a retreat, from *Jane Eyre*.' Discuss.

c. 'Social and political change are often explored and imagined through the representation of relationships between the sexes.' Discuss in relation to *Jane Eyre* and *Wide Sargasso Sea*.

Identify the key terms in each question, and then use this information to write a bullet-pointed plan about what you think you should include in an exam response. Once you have done this for each question check the feedback section (p. 190) to compare our responses, matching yours to ours.

Theology past exam questions – general theme: Christianity in contemporary Africa
Identify the key terms in each question, and then use this information to match each of the essay questions with one of the suggested numbered approaches below.

1. If you were an African Christian, how would you react to the accusation that Christianity is a foreign religion, alien to Africans.

2. What are the chief characteristics of Christianity in contemporary Africa?

3. Is Christianity still a "foreign" religion in Africa?

NOTE: Although each essay question requires the information to be presented in a different way, they can also give hints about what might be included in your answers to other questions.

4. Staying calm

Staying calm before and during the exam is easier said than done. However, there are things you can do to try and make sure you are prepared and in the right state of mind to be productive – rather than stressed and panicky. Having a revision timetable, which you are confident you have followed, is a good start. Similarly, practising with past papers in timed conditions can help you feel prepared for the actual exam – as long as you don't overdo it. It is not a great idea to be revising late the night before the exam – this is when the panic can set in, and make you anxious rather than confident.

Realistically, however, especially if you have a lot of exams, you may be revising the night before. In which case, there are still things you can do to make the day of the exam as easy as possible.

Preparing for exam day

- Make sure you know – before the morning of the exam – where the exam will be, and when it will start. If you have not been to the room before, go and check it out beforehand, so you know exactly where you are going and how long it will take.
- Get everything ready for the exam the night before, so you can go to bed feeling prepared. Take spare pens and a watch. You may need your student ID card. Also, make sure you know what you will not be allowed to take in – such as mobile phones and course books.
- Try to get a good night's sleep by:
  - separating your work space and sleep space
  - going to bed at a reasonable time
  - setting an alarm for the morning, rather than relying on waking up
  - writing a list of the revision you want to do in the morning if you are someone who can only feel prepared by doing last-minute work.
- Don't drink lots of coffee to stay awake – the caffeine increases anxiety and affects your ability to focus. Drinking water and eating fresh fruit and vegetables, and slow-burning foods such as nuts and seeds, will help your concentration and general health the most.
- Avoid panicky people – but seek out anyone who makes you calm and can help put things in perspective if you are feeling a bit stressed.
- Exercise can help you relax and get the endorphins running through your brain – which could give you much-needed energy for last-minute revision and the exam.

There are places you can get support if you are someone who really does get stressed before exams – your university should have both a counselling service, and Nightline (a 24-hour helpline, run by students, which you can call for any reason).

Keeping calm in the exam

- Try to avoid talking about the exam with other worried students immediately beforehand, especially if you know this sort of thing raises your anxiety level.

- Once in the exam, read over the test and plan your approach. Ascertain point values per part, time limits for each section, which question you'll start with to boost your confidence, etc.
- Don't hesitate to ask for clarification from the invigilator if you have questions about instructions, procedure, etc.
- Be clear about your job. A test is a thinking task, and your job during an exam is to think as clearly as possible based on what you currently know. Focus on your job (the thinking process) and practise letting go of what you don't control (the marking). Approach the test determined to think to the best of your ability, but also accept the limits of what you currently know as a beginner.
- Reduce anxiety with activity. If you go blank and can't think of anything to write, go on to another question or another part of the test. For an essay question, jot down anything you can recall on scrap paper to stimulate your memory and get your mind working.
- Relax yourself physically during the test, especially if you notice that you are not thinking well or your muscles are tight. Pause, put your test down, and take several slow, deep breaths. Tense and release your muscles. Do this in particular if you notice that you are worrying excessively about one problem, not reading carefully, and unable to recall information you know.
- Pay attention to the test, not to others. Don't waste time wondering how other people are doing.

● Summary

To do well in exams you need to find a set of revision strategies and exam techniques which work for you. However, this chapter has discussed more than that: if you keep on top of your work for a module from the beginning of the semester – really thinking about the issues that it raises, and keeping good track of your own thought processes and those of others – then you will be constantly preparing yourself for the exam. Tutors want to see in exams that their students have really thought about the topic, and have something interesting to say. You will be in a position to demonstrate this if you engage critically with the subject through the module, take every opportunity to talk to others about it, and plan your revision in such a way that it becomes a stimulating task in which you are learning about and developing own thoughts on a subject.

7 Life After University

● Introduction

This chapter should be helpful to you whether you have finished your degree or not. Indeed, the earlier you start to consider your life after university, the more you'll be able to take advantage of the opportunities that are afforded you on campus. If you *have* graduated already and fear that you have not given enough time and energy to future considerations, don't panic yet. There are plenty of things that you can do now in order to get where you want to be: reading this chapter is a good start.

● *Who* are you, and what do you *want*?

It would be easy to put a chapter at the end of this book called 'Getting a Job'. I could give you some tips, list some good websites, and even suggest how to write a CV. Getting a job, any old job, for most people, is relatively straightforward. Deciding what you want from your *career* is very different.

'Career' is a big word. By digging a little deeper into what it means for you personally, you will see that it soon turns into a word that is steeped in significance and meaning. The notion that 'having a career' is important has been drummed into us since we were kids, and forms an integral part of Western culture (whether we like it or not). 'What do you want to be when you grow up?' is such a common question asked of children, that we often overlook its deeper significance. 'What do you want to *be?*' not 'What do you want to spend your working hours *doing*?'. Your *identity* – how you perceive yourself, and how others perceive you – will be intimately tied up with what you choose to do. It is *no wonder* then that, confronted with such seemingly momentous decisions and weighed down with all that cultural baggage, many students and graduates (and people at all other stages of life, too) can feel overwhelmed.

I don't mean to scare you. The fact is that you have already embarked on your career, and you are not starting from scratch. Who you are is already being defined by the choices that you have already made. What you study, where you study; the values to which you are committed, be they religious, political, social; your life and work experiences; your particular tastes, interests and talents: all these things make you individually *you*. So, if you feel that you are struggling under the weight of seemingly limitless possibility about your future plans, and do not know where to start, take comfort from the fact that you have *already* taken steps and made choices that will help you towards a fulfilling career: a career that will be consistent with your values, that will take advantage of your skills and talents, and in which you will have an active interest. But sometimes it takes sitting down and writing about yourself to realise where you should concentrate your efforts. If you are using a scatter-gun approach and pursuing every possible lead, then you are not using your time judiciously, and you will reduce the amount of time that you can spend thinking about and preparing for a career that will really suit you.

But know that things have changed in the world of work: gone are the days when you leave university and enter a job for life. Some people find this lack of security worrying. But perhaps you could view it as liberating too: you have the flexibility to change direction, find new interests and discover untapped talent. You have a **portfolio of skills** that you can develop and bring to bear on many different employment opportunities. You are responsible for your own learning, development and growth, and you must be the person to determine your career path, wherever it may lead. First things first, though. Where are you at now? What makes you stand out from the crowd?

● You are distinctive

How do you think employers view Arts graduates? Which words spring to mind when you compare, say, an Arts graduate with someone who has studied a more scientific or business-oriented discipline? Is it a positive comparison? Is it a neutral one? Let's take one step back. How do you view *yourself* and your qualification? What comparisons or judgements do *you* make? Do you value your degree and the skills that you have developed? I have met some Arts students who have been rather disparaging about their own discipline and have described their subjects in the following terms:

"It has absolutely no bearing on real life…"
"Compared with Business or Sciences, the Arts are seen as easy, soft, wishy-washy, opinion-based and irrelevant…"
"I loved the subject, but now I need to go and get some useful skills."

You may have had these kinds of thoughts yourself. This type of attitude fascinates me, because it is held by students who are often very bright, conscientious and self-reflective. They are good students, they do well in their assessments, they are confident and articulate within their chosen discipline, and yet they singularly fail to see the impressive array of talents and skills at their disposal which their degrees have nurtured. They have failed to see how they have developed personally, socially and intellectually over the course of their three or four years at university.

So, if you are one of these individuals who find it hard to stand back and recognise how you have changed and developed, take a moment to think, now, to look backwards and ask what sort of a person you were when you began your course. Have you changed at all? In what ways? You might think that this sounds horribly patronising: it is not intended to be. Sometimes, we need the space to think about these quite fundamental questions. Of course, it is true that you are the same person as when you began your degree: you will still have many of the same traits and dispositions. But in other ways, you will have changed dramatically. How can you **identify** and **articulate** what makes you distinctive, now, as an Arts and Humanities student or graduate? Can you express what it is that you have accomplished: how you have developed, and changed, and grown? If you find it hard (and it *is* hard) to articulate why you are special, then you are going to find it very difficult to convince an employer that you are distinctive.

Those of you who say to employers that you chose the Arts merely because of your love of the subject do yourselves a disservice. It might be true that this passion is what motivated your choice, but the high-level skills that you have developed, the person that you have become via your pursuit of the subject – an enquiring, interested, critically-engaged person – these are things that you value too, right? And they are most certainly the sorts of skills that an employer will value – above and beyond a commitment to a particular subject.

● What can you do with an arts degree?

A degree in the Arts and Humanities opens the doors to many different career paths. If you are looking at formal graduate schemes in the UK, many of them do not require a specific degree discipline, but they *do* require you to be able to demonstrate particular skills and aptitudes, and to have achieved certain academic standards (for example a particular number of UCAS points or degree classification). So too with other jobs that may not be advertised through the formal graduate campaigns: the jobs advertised in local and national newspapers, or on websites such as www.monster.co.uk or www.totaljobs.com, in recruitment consultancies and also the 'hidden' opportunities that may not get advertised in newspapers or online (more on these later). Your good academic credentials show that you are intelligent and hard working: it is up to you to demonstrate that you fulfil the other criteria for which employers are looking.

Some of the fields that are open to you are:

Accountant	Management Consultant
Advertising Executive	Policy Adviser
Arts Administrator	Project Manager
Barrister	Publicist
Buyer	Publisher
Campaigns Manager	Research Assistant
Civil Servant	Sales Manager
Communications Officer	Social Worker
Copy Editor	Solicitor
Curator	Teacher
Investment Banker	Translator
Journalist	Trainer
Law	TV Producer
Lecturer	Volunteer Co-ordinator
Local Government	Writer

Identifying your skills

You *will* have developed a large set of academic and transferable skills which help you in your subsequent working life. Identifying exactly what those skills are takes some real thought. Let's make a start and try to flesh it out a little. It's easy to draw up lists of skills and attributes, and rattle them off like ingredients in a recipe – 'how to make somebody employable'. But this journey of self-discovery, or whatever you want to call it, needs to be personal and it needs to be specific. What are *your* high-level skills: can you **identify** and **articulate** them in a way that will prepare *you* for the 'real world'?

You may have been encouraged to keep a Personal Development Plan (PDP), to help you reflect upon the various skills you have developed throughout your degree. If you have a PDP and have been keeping it up to date, great. You will find it a useful document to draw upon when completing job applications and writing your CV. If you have completed your PDP in a half-hearted manner because it was merely a requirement of your personal tutorial meeting (many students tell me that this is the case), then you need to start afresh and have a good think about what your degree has equipped you with. Below are some thoughts of mine. Of course, I don't know you, so not all of these things will apply directly. However, I am quite confident that you will be able to demonstrate, to a greater or lesser extent, many of the skills that I outline below.

● Intellectual skills

Intellectual skills can be understood as critical, analytical, synthesising, and problem-solving skills. Disciplines within the Arts and Humanities ask a lot, intellectually, of students. The majority of the work that you are assessed on, as we have seen in this book, is about your independent, critical analyses of texts, theories or artefacts. You have not just been assessed on your analyses, but on the communication of these, too: through the written word, or through oral presentation.

Recognise this feeling?

Have you ever made a new, intellectual discovery? Perhaps you have been thinking hard about a particular subject, in order to write an essay or exam. You have been trying to get your thoughts in order: walking down corridors and around mazes in your brain, going over your books and notes, thinking back to lectures, groping for words, images or metaphors through which to articulate your thoughts, so that your analysis will arrange itself into some semblance of coherence. And then, all of a sudden, a wonderful, satisfying ... CLICK! The pieces all slide into place. You get it! You can see how your argument is going to fit together. (Quick, write it down before it slips away!)

That feeling, that 'eureka moment', as I shall call it – when light dawns – may not be, as in the case of Archimedes' original eureka moment, about the discovery of some great new theory. Indeed, it may only be the very smallest of insights. It may be completely personal to you; others may *never* see the world in the way that you do. Or alternatively, it may seem *banal* to other people – easily grasped and not worth remarking upon. It doesn't matter. What matters is that something has happened in *your* brain; a new piece of knowledge has been created for you and, what is more, it is entirely of your own making. You have produced it, through your own intellectual ability.

Eureka moments like these, no matter what the subject, will be the things that stay with you when you leave university, the moments that you will find the most satisfying intellectually. I believe they are what form the essence of Arts and Humanities degrees, as they exemplify what it means to think independently, critically, and with an intellectual ambition that you reach for when you are in the midst of an academic conundrum. These are what is so exciting about Arts degrees, and, even if you are still at a very early stage in your academic development, you will no doubt recognise at least something about what I am trying to describe.

The mental dexterity that you develop whilst you are studying requires ongoing practice. You might never get the chance again to think about such difficult, theoretical problems as the ones you do at university. You have learned what is required in your course (and hopefully this book has been some help to you, too), but you might not realise that the skills that you have been developing are the sorts of thing that you need to keep well-honed. Arts degrees are wonderful sharpeners of the mind; you are alert to arguments, to reasoning, to evidence, to texts, to images, and you are able to engage with world-renowned experts on subjects that are not accessible to much of the general population. But this sharpness can be dulled, can be lost without practice. Be sure to maintain your abilities: by thinking critically, by reading, by listening to current affairs, by continuing to push yourself intellectually, even when there is no essay deadline or exam looming.

Why do I say this? Why do I not say, give yourself a break after all that hard work and study? Well, a break is a good idea – a holiday from the stress and the deadlines and the exam rooms is well-earned, I'm sure. Just don't make it a permanent break. The critical abilities that you have learned and developed, that have led to your very own eureka moments, are the very abilities that employers want. Your independence of mind – the ability to step back and approach an issue from many different perspectives is exactly the sort of skill that is invaluable in highly complex organisations. If you are to be a leader of the future (and why not?), no matter what the industry or profession, you will need to be able to critically assess where you and your organisation are going and why; you should be able to see the long term and the short term and predict obstacles and propose solutions. A person with a sharp mind, one willing to question received wisdom and come up with new answers, taking in all the evidence and the relevant information, would be a very useful contributor to an organisation.

● Communication skills

So, you've got great intellectual abilities when it comes to critical analysis. But, as you know from the feedback that you have received on your assessments, ideas and arguments aren't worth much if you are unable to communicate them clearly. You may have heard reports in the media that employers bemoan a lack of basic writing skills from new graduates. *Your* degree is likely to have been weighted heavily towards written communication, so hopefully you are relatively strong in this regard: you've had plenty of opportunities to practise. If you *do* lack confidence in your written skills, there are places on campus that will be able to help you. Ask your personal tutor to refer you to the right place, if you are unsure where to look.

Written communication

You've had a chance to practise your written skills, through the vehicle of essays, reports and exams, but these academic assignments form just one type of written communication. Essays, in particular, are peculiar in their rigid formality and in the fact that their intended audience is usually expert. You will find that employers are looking for a range of writing styles that go beyond the academic; you need to be able to demonstrate that you are confident in writing for different purposes and for different audiences. Here's a list of some of the ways you might be asked to write. They are organised in two separate categories, external and internal communications, in order to reflect whether the intended audience is within the company itself, or outside. With which of these are you comfortable and familiar? How many have you read yourself, or even written?

External written communications

These are written for audiences beyond the company or organisation, for example, customers, general public, industry regulators.

The **internet**, of course, doesn't have just one style, but all websites *do* need to be direct, easily understood and jargon-free. Organisations vary enormously in how they present themselves online, as this is a key method of communicating their individual profile. Compare the written content of the web pages of three different organisations. How do they differ in their tone and in their presentation? Who is their intended audience? What message are these organisations trying to get across? Here are three to get you started:

A fruit drink manufacturer

Innocent Ltd   http://www.innocentdrinks.co.uk/us [accessed 07.06.09]

our story

We had good jobs before we started innocent. Why did we change?

our vehicles

Some of our vans are cows and some are grass-covered ones that dance. Obviously.

careers at innocent

Looking for a job? Why not come and work at innocent?

our ethics

We sure aren't perfect, but we're trying to do the right thing.

join the family

Join our family to get our newsletter and lots of other nice free stuff.

contact us

Call the banana phone, or just have a look at some bad pictures of us.

© 2009 Innocent Drinks

A government department

Home Office

http://www.homeoffice.gov.uk/about-us/purpose-and-aims [accessed 07.06.09]

Our purpose

Working together to protect the public

We put public protection very clearly at the heart of our work to counter terrorism, cut crime, provide effective policing, secure our borders and protect personal identity.

Our strategy

We want people to feel safe, and confident in their homes and neighbourhoods, so they can live freely, contribute to society and prosper in their daily lives. The Home Office strategy sets out our direction for the next three years for the full range of our work.

Read what we plan to achieve, how we plan to achieve it, and the measures we will use to assess our progress in the Home Office Strategy.

© Crown copyright 2009

An investment bank

Goldman Sachs

http://www2.goldmansachs.com/our-firm/about-us/business-principles.
html [accessed 07.06.09]

The Goldman Sachs Business Principles

1. Our clients' interests always come first. Our experience shows
    that if we serve our clients well, our own success will follow.

2. Our assets are our people, capital and reputation. If any of these
    is ever diminished, the last is the most difficult to restore. We are
    dedicated to complying fully with the letter and spirit of the laws,
    rules and ethical principles that govern us. Our continued success
    depends upon unswerving adherence to this standard.

3. Our goal is to provide superior returns to our shareholders.
    Profitability is critical to achieving superior returns, building our
    capital and attracting and keeping our best people. Significant
    employee stock ownership aligns the interests of our employees
    and our shareholders.

You can see, very quickly, that styles vary just in this one medium. How flexible is your writing style? Have you ever published work on the web? Did you find it easy or difficult? Writing for the web is not as straightforward as it may seem.

Marketing literature and advertising copy, like the web, is crucial to a company's commercial success. You may have developed marketing skills in your part-time job, involvement in a society, lobbying group, or sports team. Examples of advertising material include press releases, posters, leaflets, flyers, email shots and 'viral' internet-based adverts.

Funding bids and project proposals are of vital importance for organisations, such as charities, non-governmental organisations (NGOs), or consultancies, that rely on external funding. Your ability to write clearly and persuasively in formal funding applications will be crucial. This type of writing is one that requires practice; the best way to learn is through reading examples of successful applications that have gone before.

Email will be crucial in your work life, wherever you are employed. Whether you are communicating with internal colleagues or external clients, always err on the side of formality, until you are sure of the company's written style conventions. Begin with 'Dear'; do not use abbreviations, slang, jargon or txtspk; punctuate as you would in a letter and sign off courteously with 'Regards' or 'Best wishes'. If you are **applying for a job** via email make sure your **email address** gives the right impression about you. For example, addresses such as drunkagain@hotmail.com or princesstalula@aol.com do not present a professional or favourable image!

Industry magazines or journals will present an external 'face' of the company to the sector. Of course, how a company communicates with other organisations within its industry will depend on a number of factors, not least, whether it is in competition with them or not.

Internal written communications

These are written for audiences within the company or organisation, for example, team members, senior managers, directors, shareholders.

Project proposals will require clarity and precision, outlining the aims of the project, the names of all the parties involved, the budget breakdown, the project's intended results, performance indicators and a timeline of when and how it is to be delivered.

Reports, position papers and executive summaries will also require clarity, drawing out relevant details and presenting them succinctly. Reports with numerical data might include graphical representation, percentages, or spreadsheets. Executive summaries give a synopsis at the start of a report, headlining any key results, findings or conclusions. You may have had to write an abstract for your dissertation: executive summaries function in a similar way.

Minutes of meetings will vary in style, so be sure to check for a style guide (or, at the very least, read old minutes to see how they were done). Usually, minutes are phrased in the past tense, are anonymised, and include numbered paragraphs that may continue from the previous meeting. If you are new to taking minutes, make sure you know the names of everyone in the room, and draw a plan of where they were sitting round the table to help you remember who said what. You'll need to be able to write clearly and quickly, and to be able to understand your own abbreviations when writing up!

Committee papers are formally written documents that are to be considered by the committee: check the formal procedures for circulation with the committee secretary, together with any formatting and linguistic conventions.

Oral communication

Students and graduates often tend to think of PowerPoint™ presentations when asked to consider an occasion when they have demonstrated skills of 'oral communication'. That's odd, because formal presentations like these are only one, very particular, and not everyday, form of communication. There are many ways – beyond Powerpoint – in which you'll be asked to communicate orally. Table 7.1 shows a sample of some of the tasks that you may be asked to perform, together with some of the skills that you need in order to be able to perform the tasks effectively. The tasks get less formal from top to bottom, but this does *not* mean that they get less *important*.

● Interpersonal skills

Hand-in-hand with skills of oral communication, as can be seen, are interpersonal skills. Companies and organisations need employees who can get on with a wide variety of people, sometimes under difficult and stressful conditions! Your ability to **work as part of a team** is crucial. This means that you can get on with people, understand where they are coming from, empathise with their point of view and show respect. It also means contributing to team morale, by being motivated, committed and willing to come up with new ideas. This motivation and enthusiasm makes a world of difference in a team environment. Equally, if you are **leading** or **managing** a team or project, your interpersonal skills will be called on to an even greater extent. Amongst other things, you will need to be able win people's trust, persuade others to your point of view, have confidence in your ideas, and negotiate deadlines or agreements. These are all high-level skills that require an ability to establish rapport with a wide range of people, whether senior managers, team members or clients.

● Organisational skills

Being organised pays dividends in the workplace, not only for your own efficiency, but for the effectiveness of the organisation at large. Of course, employers know this, so many ask new recruits to be able to demonstrate

Type of oral communication	Skills required
Presentations to an external or internal audience	Ability to control voice: pace, volume and tone; enthusiasm; use of engaging content and appropriate visual props; able to respond to questions
Pitching a product to an investor	Enthusiasm, confidence, knowledge
Introducing a new project to the Board	Motivation; able to respond to criticism positively
Training staff	Ability to adopt a flexible pace; clarity; ability to meet the individual needs of staff
Reporting findings at a meeting	Clarity; succinctness
Defending a point of view on a committee	Knowledge; confidence; negotiation skills
Managing a team; conducting staff reviews	Ability to gain trust; discretion; fairness; build rapport; able to give constructive criticism; empathy; ability to negotiate an agreement
One-to-one conversations with managers, team members, customers, volunteers, face to face/ telephone	Awareness of others' perspectives; friendliness; ability to sell a product or an idea; able to receive constructive criticism; enthusiasm
Small meetings with colleagues	Timeliness; preparedness; focus; sense of humour; friendliness; motivation
Contribution to a team dynamic	Sense of humour; helpfulness; motivation; enthusiasm
Socialising with colleagues during lunch break or after work	Friendliness; sense of humour; ability to talk to a wide variety of people

Table 7.1   Communication skills

organisational skills in CVs and applications. Think about the way in which you have organised your time at university: how would you describe it? How have you handled the competing pressures of getting work finished, preparing for seminars, enjoying your social life? Chaotic? Stressful? Organised? Planned?

In your work life, just as in your time at university, you will be trusted with a great deal of autonomy in organising your days, weeks, months and years. However, whereas at uni you were only really answering to yourself to get things done, at work you will be accounting for your time to a manager or employer. You'll need to be able to demonstrate that you can organise and motivate yourself to complete work, even when no one is looking over your shoulder. You'll also need to be able to demonstrate that you can prioritise so that you can complete tasks which compete for time and resources.

How can you show a potential employer that you can **organise your time, prioritise your work**, so that you can **plan, execute and deliver a project** over the short, medium and long term? Here are some suggestions: some of them you might already do as a matter of course; others you might consider adopting in future.

Organising your time

- A diary, calendar or PDA for meetings, events, deadlines.
- Shared online calendars and meeting organisers, such as Microsoft Outlook™
- Keep your desk, desktop and office tidy! Establish a system for ordering your files.
- Attend meetings fully prepared: what do you need to get out of them? Perhaps you could draw up an agenda so that your time is used efficiently.

Prioritising work

- Find out deadlines and work cycles.
- Communicate with colleagues – how does your work fit into the bigger picture?
- Rank work in order of importance, and in order of length of time to complete.

Planning projects

- Draw up a tentative timescale, indicating each stage of the project.
- Monitor by using 'project milestones', e.g. 'By 1st December, we will have completed X, by 10th January we will have completed Z.'
- Predict 'indicators of success', e.g. 'We will know that the project has been a success because we can measure its impact by...'

● Research skills

When employers ask for research skills they may have a different idea to the one that you have in mind, so tread carefully here. With a degree in the Arts and Humanities you will, more than likely, have used research skills when writing essays and reports, by using libraries and databases, and, to a lesser extent, the internet. You may also have had the opportunity to research a more extended piece of work in the form of a final-year dissertation. You may have received training on bibliographical or practical methods that were necessary for the completion of a project. Academic enquiry is one sort of research, and requires understanding of a subject and the ability to critically analyse it. Find out whether this is the type of research that your potential employer is looking for, by reading the job description carefully, or by simply asking. Some research roles require both *qualitative* and *quantitative* research: data collection in a particular field and possibly a statistical analysis of the results. Other research roles, for example, a *Television Researcher*, will rely on finding information from individuals over the telephone.

● Numeracy

Employers need staff who are numerate as well as literate. In fact, many of the large graduate recruiters actually ask applicants to take a numeracy test as part of the recruitment process. As an Arts and Humanities graduate, you might feel a little bit anxious at the thought of taking a numerical reasoning test. If you are a graduate in your early twenties, it might have been over five years since you last had to think about a maths exam. If you absolutely *hate* working with numbers, then you're unlikely to be pursuing a career, say, as a statistician. However, you *will* need to brush up on the basics, such as fractions and percentages if you intend to apply to a formal graduate scheme.

There is no need to panic just yet, though. Since leaving school you will have had many opportunities to demonstrate your numerical abilities, even without noticing; you may just need to re-familiarise yourself with some first principles. 'Brain-train' games and old textbooks might offer some help, but by far the most useful method is to do some practice tests. Your Careers Service will be able to provide you with tests, or tell you where you can find them online. The key to success is through practising under *timed conditions*. The more you practise, the quicker you'll become; this is crucial because graduate recruiters often put too many questions in their tests, to see how many you can get through in the allotted time. The usual advice is to quickly assess whether you'll be able to answer correctly: if not, leave it and move on to the next question. Before you adopt this method, check whether the questions are weighted, so that they get harder/earn you more points as you progress. Don't be afraid to ask as many questions about the practicalities of the exam as you need: you won't be deducted any marks.

Beyond the application process, you will also need your numerical, mathematical or financial skills within the workplace such as:

- Manipulating and presenting data in spreadsheets and databases (e.g. Microsoft Excel™ and Access™).
- Analysing information and forming decisions.
- Developing knowledge of the financial conditions under which you are working. For example, having an idea of the company's turnover, profit/loss, sales, targets, monthly and annual financial reports, even if you are not working directly with financial data on a day-to-day basis.

Commercial awareness

Academics and students in the Arts and Humanities are sometimes accused of having an 'Ivory Tower' mentality – cutting themselves off from the world of business and commerce and concentrating solely on their academic world of library and lecture theatre. This is an attitude to guard against, if you want a career beyond academia! Employers, no matter what the sector, want to hire graduates who are *genuinely interested* in their industry and who can demonstrate *enthusiasm* for their product or service. Interest and enthusiasm go a long way in looking attractive to employers, but this must be supported by some real *knowledge*. If you are applying for jobs and feel you don't know much about the company, organisation or industry, then do some basic research before you send off your application. The company's website is a good place to start, but for a broader understanding, you will need to find magazines, journals or newspaper supplements that focus on the particular sector.

There is a wealth of information available to you on websites and in newspapers. If you feel that you are still sketchy on some points, then try to gain some experience within the sector at which you are looking. Even if this is merely work-shadowing for a few days, or helping for a few hours a week on a voluntary basis, any experience which demonstrates an active interest in, and enthusiasm for, the particular industry is going to be beneficial.

Commercial awareness checklist

How much do you know about the company or organisation?

- Product/service
- Competitors/rivals
- Market conditions
- Industry/sector current news or issues
- International/national presence
- Company profile, character or history

Summary of skills – analysing your portfolio

Figure 7.1 is a checklist of employment skills – use it to analyse your own portfolio of skills.

Filling in the skills gaps

Look at the summary of skills in Figure 7.1. It's a long list. No one expects you to be able to demonstrate *all* of these when you first graduate, and no *individual job* will require all of them, but you will need to be able to demonstrate some of them, if you intend to enter the world of work. Whether you have an idea about a career you are interested in or not, you will need to look critically at your own list of attributes, and assess whether there are any major gaps in your portfolio.

Start by being positive: write down where your *strengths* lie. Which skills do you *know* you have, and can demonstrate? Which areas do feel comfortable with? Perhaps you are a 'people' person and like to talk on the phone; maybe you are meticulous and systematic and enjoy sifting through complex written information; perhaps you have a passion for a particular type of industry and know it inside out. Whatever your strengths, write down a few sentences expanding on what you are good at and why. Try to think of one or two examples that demonstrate that strength. When you've done this, take some time to think about what you *don't* feel comfortable with: don't be too hard on yourself, but try to think honestly about your skills. Maybe you just haven't yet had the opportunity to work in the particular sector that interests you; perhaps you are nervous about public-speaking (don't worry, many people are); maybe you need to gain experience of working in a team environment, or perhaps you've never taken on a 'leadership' role.

Skill	How do I rate? Strong/Weak?	How can I demonstrate it? Think of an example
Intellectual Skills e.g. critical analysis, problem solving		
Written Communication e.g. reports, websites, minutes, projects, adverts		
Oral Communication e.g. defend a point of view, give a presentation		
Interpersonal Skills e.g. establish rapport with a variety of people		
Leadership Skills e.g. come up with an idea and win trust, take responsibility		
Management Skills e.g. delegate tasks, gain confidence		
Team-working e.g. contribute ideas, 'muck in'		
Organisation e.g. plan and monitor work		
Research e.g. use databases effectively		
Numeracy e.g. work with numbers confidently, present graphical information		
Commercial Awareness e.g. understanding of a sector, specific knowledge of an organisation		

Figure 7.1   Portfolio of skills

If you do have an idea – no matter how vague – of the type of work in which you are interested, you can do a lot to help yourself fill in the gaps of your skills profile. Find job adverts and read the person specification – the criteria that you must meet in order to be short-listed for an interview. Very often, this will be divided into 'essential' and 'desirable' characteristics. Compare similar job adverts from more than one company – are they each asking for the same experience and skills? You will need to demonstrate that you meet all of the essential criteria if you are get through to the next round. If you think you are lacking in a particular area, then you need to think creatively about the ways in which you can fill in some of the gaps in your portfolio of skills and experiences. You could, for example:

- Enrol in an evening class (e.g. introduction to databases/web authoring).
- Work shadow for a week in a company/sector that interests you.
- Join a local organisation or political group.
- Volunteer to be on the management committee of a small charity.
- Take a leadership role in a sports team.
- Become a learning mentor at a local school.
- Apply for an internship in the company you want to work for.
- Suggest you take on more/different responsibility in your part-time job.

Articulating your talents

You've done the hard part and acquired your skills, whether through your academic curriculum, or through your co-curricular activities, such as part-time work, involvement in sport, politics and societies, or experience in the voluntary sector. Now you need to 'sell' yourself and your skills to employers. Now is not the time for modesty, no matter if you are naturally shy or retiring. Now is the time to be proud of your achievements and articulate them in such a way that employers will sit up and listen! There is no need to feel that you have to over-exaggerate either; the trick is to articulate your talents in a way that employers can relate to, and show that you understand what it is they are looking for. Whether through the written word, in the form of CVs and application forms, or face-to-face in interviews, your contact with employers is key and should be approached with care.

The application process

Sending a **curriculum vitae** (CV), together with a covering letter, remains a common format when applying for certain sorts of job. If you are considering applying for jobs *beyond* formal graduate recruitment schemes (which tend to use application forms), then you should begin to consider drawing up your own CV. There are many places online that give advice: a good place to find examples of different kinds of CVs is www.prospects.ac.uk. Your careers service will also be able to provide you with examples too. One of the most important things to remember when writing a CV is that you should **tailor it** for each new job. Sending out the *same* CV to different employers, who ask for *different* skills and experience, will not get you very far: you need to present your CV in a way that will appeal to an employer's specific priorities, requirements and ethos.

- Remember always to **use examples** of occasions when you have demonstrated particular skills.
- Try to **vary** examples so that they are not all from the same period.
- Use **action words** and **bullet points** rather than just listing previous roles and responsibilities. For example:
  - ○ 'Achieved...'
  - ○ 'Was responsible for...',
  - ○ 'Lead a team...'
  - ○ 'Initiated...'
  - ○ 'Created...'
  - ○ 'Was successful in...'
  - ○ 'Made profit...'
  - ○ 'Produced...'
  - ○ 'Contributed...'
  - ○ 'Managed...'
  - ○ 'Negotiated...'

Once you have had a go at writing your CV, **show it to someone** and get some feedback. This might be a careers adviser at your university's careers service, or it might just be someone whom you trust, or who has some work experience. Ask for feedback on the formatting as well as the content: is it *easy to read* and *does it make sense* to an outsider? Like writing an essay, you should expect to re-draft several times.

Application forms present their own particular challenges. Again, your best source of advice will be your careers service. Make an appointment with an adviser once you have had a first go at completing an application form – preferably well before the deadline, so that you can amend and re-draft in light of any comments an adviser may make. In addition, you will certainly need to research carefully the organisation to which you are apply-ing (see **Commercial Awareness Checklist** (p. 174)). You may find that the organisation itself provides you with guidelines or tips in completing the application form. Ensure that you have read as much of this information as possible before you begin. You need to be able to understand the character of the organisation and the sort of person that they are looking for; equally, you need to know whether *it* as a company is a good match for *you*.

Many organisations use **competency-based questions** on their appli-cations. These forms typically ask you to give examples of occasions when you have demonstrated a particular skill or attribute. For example, you may come across questions such as:

Give an example of a time when you...

...overcame an obstacle to achieve a result.
...played an active role in a team.
...challenged a received idea.
...presented an idea to senior colleagues.
...persuaded someone to see your point of view.
...delivered an objective under pressure.
...showed determination.
...coped well with change.
...made a difficult decision.

These types of questions are designed to give employers a picture of your skills profile: your personality, talents and attributes – and, of course, to see whether you can write clearly and persuasively too. You can see that they **do not ask for specific work experience**, but they *do* ask you to think crea-tively about *all* your experiences, whether academic or from extra-curricular activities such as sport, travel or voluntary work.

There is a good way to answer these questions, a way that sets out clearly for the employer exactly what you have achieved and how. It is called the **CAR** approach, and stands for **Context-Action-Result**.

CONTEXT: What was the situation? What were you trying to achieve? What was *your* role?
ACTION: What action did *you* take personally? What skills did you use?
RESULT: What was the outcome? Was it a success? What did you learn? What would you do differently?

Always write in the *first person*. An employer needs to know what *you* did, and what skills *you* demonstrated, even if your example involves a group or a team. Be specific about outcomes, and if the result wasn't a complete success show that you learnt from any mistakes that you might have made.

Interviews

Articulating your skills and talents on paper is one thing: in person it can feel quite different. When you are invited to an interview or an assessment day, try to relax as much as possible. This is, of course, very easy to say, but less easy to do in practice. There are things that you can do to help you be in the best frame of mind possible:

- Take time to consider possible questions beforehand.
- Practise talking about yourself to someone else (sometimes difficult, but gets easier the more you do it!).
- Know where you are going: try to visit the location beforehand.
- Get to the venue early.
- Have written information of who you are meeting and time of appointment.
- Get an early night and don't drink alcohol the night before.
- Try some relaxation techniques immediately beforehand: breathe slowly through your nose; relax the muscles in your face; smile.

During the interview, one of the most important things that you must do is *presume the employer knows nothing about you*. Of course, they may have read your CV or application, but they may not have had time to read it in any detail. Besides, they may have read hundreds of applications for the same job. The interview is your chance to talk positively about yourself and about your skills and experience. **Structure your answers**, so that they make sense and use appropriate examples like you did in your application. Again, you can use the **Context-Action-Result** method in order to articulate your achievements. If you dry up, and are stuck for words, take a moment to think rather than start babbling.

> Remember that for the interviewer, it's just another day at the office. This thought might help you to calm down and relax a little.

As well as thinking about what you say, consider your body language: are you projecting an interested, enthusiastic, motivated and friendly persona? Slumping in your chair, twiddling with your hair, not making eye contact and not smiling will not do you any favours. Conversely, staring down your interviewer with a fixed grin will also give the wrong impression. If you are polite, friendly and smiling and you respond to what your interviewer is saying with interest, you will be on the right track.

Any questions?

The interview is also your chance to find out more about the job and the organisation: you should definitely go prepared with questions about the company or its work. This will not only be useful to you when you are deciding if you really want to accept a position, but it will also demonstrate to the employer that you have done some research about the company and are genuinely knowledgeable and interested. Don't just ask about the salary or the benefits on offer: this will not give the right impression!

Further study

If you loved your time at university, and relished the opportunities for learning and personal development that you found there, you may be considering returning to study after you graduate. Continuing your development for its own sake, within your chosen discipline is a rewarding experience in itself. Alternatively, you may wish to gain a specific postgraduate degree which will qualify you for a particular profession. Examples include law 'conversion courses', librarianship diplomas, teaching (PGCE), curatorial studies and journalism diplomas. Some of these, such as the law conversion course, are mandatory for you to be considered in that profession. Others are simply options that may increase your chance of finding work in that sector. Your Careers Service should be able to help choose the right course and institution for you, and will be able to guide you through any funding or scholarship applications that are available.

Travel and time out

Taking time out to travel after you graduate, if you are able to manage the financial burden, is a great idea. If you are unsure about what you want to do, or simply want some time to get away from it all, then independent travel is an option which will broaden your outlook, enhance your coping and survival skills, create opportunities and give you ideas about your future direction. Many graduates combine independent travel with working or volunteering abroad. This is a great way to fill some of the gaps in your CV, and demonstrates to future employers that you have balanced fun, adventure and some serious work. There are many companies, organisations and charities that are looking for graduate volunteers abroad. A popular choice is Teaching English as a Foreign Language (TEFL). The British Council recruits Language Assistants for posts throughout the world – usually language undergraduates or graduates with an interest in teaching. Other Language schools might require a TEFL qualification, or equivalent. Some private companies promise work experience abroad in highly competitive industries such as TV, radio or journalism. Be wary of those companies that charge a high price for this 'opportunity'. Very often the package does not include the price of long-distance flights, or other transfers. Do some research into what the work will actually involve, the hours that you will put in, and whether there is any support for you locally. Remember too that there are many charities and NGOs who rely on the support of volunteers for their existence; these organisations will not charge you for the opportunity to work for them, but they will require you to be committed and motivated.

Searching for a job, finding a career

This chapter has discussed the many different types of skills that you will have developed during your university career – whether within a discipline itself, or through co-curricular activities and part-time employment. Where you choose to apply these skills, of course, is up to you: an Arts and Humanities degree will equip you for just about anything. Opportunities for graduate work will be advertised on your campus: at recruitment fairs, in your careers service, on websites such as www.prospects.ac.uk and in newspapers such as *The Guardian* on Saturdays.

Hidden opportunities

If you are interested in careers that don't seem to be advertised anywhere (for example TV, media, journalism and publishing), remember that graduate recruitment schemes and jobs websites are only part of the market. For highly competitive jobs (where employers don't need to spend thousands of pounds on recruitment campaigns and advertising) there *are* opportunities to be found, it might just take a bit more digging. Your networking skills will be crucial to finding these opportunities: many graduates fear networking involves making conversation over canapés at specially organised events. There's no need to worry, if this thought fills you with trepidation. The best kind of networking often means talking to people that you already know.

Think about your friends, family or friends of your parents: who has a job that you like the sound of, or works in an industry in which you are interested? How easy would it be to give them a call or meet up for a coffee to discuss how they got their job? Most people will be happy to talk about their own career and give advice to people who want to follow similar routes. Don't be afraid to ask whether they know of any opportunities for paid work or voluntary work experience. At the very least, they will have you in mind if they hear of anything in future.

Getting started

At the start of this chapter I said that finding a career is not just a matter of searching for a job. That's true, a career *is* more than that, but it may *also* be the case that you only discover what you want your career to be after you've had a few jobs, ruled out certain options or discovered new passions. Very few people embark on their ideal career as soon as they leave university, so don't be disappointed if you don't. There are huge advantages to engaging in short-term work or temping jobs: they can often lead to longer-term employment and give you a taste of an industry, whilst at the same time expanding your knowledge and skills portfolio. Don't be scared to try a few different things out, or to head in a new direction if you find that something's not for you. There are many opportunities out there available to you, given your many talents and abilities: it's time to get started and discover what they are. Good luck!

● Resources

- http://www.prospects.ac.uk [accessed 07.06.09]
  This is a fantastic resource aimed at graduates and students. It includes graduate jobs and work experience, online forums, advice and sample CVs.
- http://www.milkround.com [accessed 07.06.09]
  The 'milkround' was what graduate employers called the Careers Fairs at universities. This site brings the milkround up to date, advertising graduate jobs and internships and also offering useful hints and tips.
- http://www.totaljobs.com [accessed 07.06.09]
  This is a general search engine for any type of job in the UK. There is a specific Graduate category.
- http://jobs.guardian.co.uk/ [accessed 07.06.09]
  This is *The Guardian* newspaper's online job search facility, which includes a range of sectors. It is particularly strong in the areas of Media, Culture and Education.

- http://www.britishcouncil.org [accessed 07.06.09]
  Find opportunities for teaching English language abroad.
- Graduate Careers Fairs.
- National and local newspapers.
- Your university Careers Service and library.

Summary

This chapter has asked you to think carefully about your own personal development – what you have achieved, the skills that you have acquired and the knowledge that you have gained during your degree. Facing the prospect of life after university, no matter what your age or background, can be daunting. Indeed, the idea of 'having a career' comes with a lot of cultural baggage, which might be off-putting. But remember, you are not starting from scratch: you have already made choices that will shape your future, that are consistent with your values, interests and talents. You most likely chose an Arts and Humanities degree because of your interest in and/or aptitude for a particular subject. If you are looking at work options – and there is a wide range of sectors of work open to you – now is the time to think beyond that passion and try to *articulate* what you gained from your degree besides pleasure: what skills and knowledge have you developed? This chapter has suggested some of the types of skills that employers are looking for – intellectual skills, communication skills, organisation skills to name just a few. Your job now is to work out how you *demonstrate* these skills to employers, both in writing and in interview situations. There are a few tricks of the trade that we have suggested, including the very useful 'CAR' approach.

If you feel you are not quite ready to enter the world of work, or you need an additional qualification for a particular industry, taking time out for travel, voluntary work or further study, will not be time wasted, so long as you get yourself organised and research your options – and finances – thoroughly.

And remember, don't be disheartened if your first attempts at finding a career do not yield the results you were hoping for straight away: working out what you want to do, and getting there, can be a full-time job in itself, and will take some trial and error. Talk to friends and family, to personal tutors and careers advisers to get as much support as possible. Listen out for opportunities that might not be advertised formally, and learn how other people got their job, if you like the sound of working in that particular industry. There are opportunities out there and there are many sources of ideas, inspiration and support that will help you find them.

Feedback

● **Chapter 2**

Exercise on page 30

Website 1

Wikipedia is not sufficiently authorised for you to use it as the main source for your essay, but it can provide an overview of a subject. This Darwinism website provides some seemingly useful information, but it is not presented as a critical opinion – more as a general introduction. It might be somewhere you go to find out about Darwin before really delving into academic articles and books. It could be useful for providing references for other sources to look at. Remember to treat Wikipedia – and sites like it – with caution, however. The contributors to any 'wiki' can be anybody with internet access. They are not necessarily experts in their field. For example, you could be citing the work of a GCSE student, or a keen amateur who is basing their information on enthusiastic pub conversations alone. Although there are attempts at post-hoc moderation of content, anyone is allowed to amend most articles.

Website 2

This site is not appropriate as an academic source for an essay. The author of the article has a clear bias – writing from a primarily religious viewpoint. The evidence used to back up his points is not fully referenced and is based on Catholic doctrine, which is ultimately based on faith rather than critical reasoning.

Website 3

This article seems much more appropriate. The academic is making an argument about Darwin's influence on nineteenth-century thought, which it would be useful to draw upon and respond to in an academic essay. Moreover, if you check out the website for this article, it contains many academic articles covering different areas of Darwinism and Evolutionary Theory. These articles are written by experts in the field who use and reference evidence to support their points. This site can also lead you to many other useful sources of information. It was found using the search facility Intute.

● Chapter 3

Exercise on page 58

Example 1

Marx is writing a manifesto. This makes his writing style quite extreme. He has a clear political agenda, which he is expressing using repetition and emotive terms such as 'naked self-interest' and 'philistine sentimentalism'. This is not so much a balanced argument as a call to arms. When reading this, you would need to acknowledge that this is a political manifesto, thinking about how Marx is defining the bourgeoisie, constructing his argument through characterising them as capitalist exploiters. His extreme language, his listing, and his one-dimensional view enhance this characterisation – he is looking through the lens of economic analysis. It is there to set the scene for Marx's political agenda.

Example 2

This is an academic argument, with Hawkins using examples from every-day life to draw conclusions about how waste functions in our society, as well as show how our society functions. She also draws upon a key theorist – emphasising how important this theorist is, summing up her main contribution to the subject, but also making clear her limitations, and so showing what Hawkins can contribute to the subject. Notice as well, however, that although this passage contains some complex ideas and complicated, academic language (for example, *'it is a cultural performance, an organized sequence of material practices, that deploys certain technologies, bodily techniques and assumptions'),* she also makes an effort to sound down-to-earth. Perhaps in the same way she wants to point to the gritty materiality of waste, she doesn't want to get too carried away with using formal language and abstract ideas. Instead, she writes a little as if she is talking to a more general audience – using the everyday experience to think through what waste means. When responding to a passage like this, you could think about whether your everyday experience is similar to Hawkins', and think about whether you agree with her view of waste, more than Mary Douglas' by going to read Mary Douglas – in other words, this is a useful passage in that it gives you one of the key readings for this subject.

Example 3

This, as with all of Plato's work, is written in the form of a dialogue. When reading it, think how, by presenting his philosophical ideas as part of a discussion, Plato is able to pick apart the structure of an argument. In this passage, we see Socrates teaching Thrasymachus to make his argument more clear, by pointing out potential flaws in the way that it is first presented. This allows the reader to think about the faults in Thrasymachus's argument – but also to think about how precise a philosophical argument has to be in order to be successful. It also allows us to follow the logic one step at a time, through testing out each argument with examples. When thinking about how to respond to a passage like this, you could think of your own examples and counter-examples to test the arguments presented. It is easy to be swept along by accomplished rhetoricians like Plato; slow down and subject each step to criticism and questioning.

● Chapter 5

Exercise on page 95

Sample essay question 1

You would need to define and analyse three terms, 'Tyrant', 'Founder' and 'Europe'. What do Tyrant and Founder mean? Are they really oppositional terms as the question seems to imply? And what should we consider Europe to mean for the purposes of the question? (Should we adopt a modern concept, or use a medieval equivalent such as Christendom?)

In your plan you would also need to factor in space to outline the 'esteem' in which Charlemagne has been held, and then consider *on the one hand* how much he deserves it (this would be one section) and *on the other* how much he does not. You would then come to a conclusion which does not necessarily come down on either side, but which sums up the complexity of the situation whilst making some kind of decision (e.g. whilst Charlemagne did these good things, he was effectively a tyrant...).

In other words you need to demonstrate you have considered all aspects of the question critically and used your analytical skills to come to a conclusion.

Sample essay question 2

In answering this question you would first need to examine what the question might understand by 'German film'. This could be discussed in a number of ways. Is a 'German film' to be understood in terms of its production context, i.e. where the film was shot/how it was funded/who worked on it? Or does the 'Germanness' of a film reside in its style/thematic content/its intertextual points of reference?

A good answer might then place this discussion in the wider context of the film's critical reception, looking at how this reception reflects the problem of definition alluded to in the question.

This would then be followed by a detailed examination of the film text itself, perhaps taking each competing definition of 'German film' in turn and examining the extent to which *Run Lola Run* does or does not conform.

Finally, the essay would assess whether it is possible, or even desirable, to offer a definitive answer to the question.

Exercise on page 97

Paragraph 1 would begin:

> To the question 'What is Marxist criticism?' it may be tempting to respond with another question: 'What does it matter?'

This sentence asks two questions and the rest of the paragraph explains the importance of answering these questions.

Paragraph 2 would begin:

> In fact, however, there is no reason why Marxist criticism should weaken, let alone disappear.

This sentence connects the two paragraphs by indicating directly that this paragraph will demonstrate why the ideas of the last were limiting – Marxist criticism is still important. The sentence also serves to tell us what this paragraph will be about.

Paragraph 3 would begin:

> The argument could even be made that Marxist criticism has been strengthened by the collapse of Soviet-style communism.

This connects the final two paragraphs by indicating how the argument in the last paragraph could be taken further. The phrase 'the argument could even be made' refers back to the argument the writer made in Paragraph 2.

Exercise on page 99

Student example 1

There are good things about this introduction. It builds up a logical sequence of thoughts about storytelling in general, before moving on to *Othello*; the discussion of the different kinds of storytelling is useful. Moreover, this is quite a confident, original way to start an essay – with the student's own thoughts, rather than relying on a critical quotation. This discussion leads nicely to the Stephen Greenblatt comment, and the student demonstrates an understanding of this quotation, using it effectively to structure an argument around.

However, there are some problems. It is quite long and it takes a while to get going. The first section could have been expressed more succinctly; it begins to sound quite repetitive with the words 'story' and 'storyteller' being repeated continually. Moreover, whilst some kind of primary argument is indicated (all the characters fictionalise their own lives – this essay will focus upon Othello's tendency to 'narrative self-fashioning'), the introduction never really states what the writer's thesis is. We are left with a statement of intention: 'I would like to consider…', rather than a thesis statement 'I will demonstrate…'. One more sentence at the end of the introduction indicating what the final argument will be – or even a reworking of the material already down on paper – would help make this a much more effective introduction.

Student example 2

This is a very good, focused introduction. It *begins* with a salient quotation from the book under discussion which proves an effective way to both introduce the main topic of the essay, and demonstrate the student's understanding of the question. The student continues to explore the terms of the question – making clear how the metaphor of 'nets' will be used. It is a pity, however, that the important distinction between 'those who truly find themselves and those who fail to fly by' is put in brackets, as if an afterthought. The whole introduction is used to outline the essay's argument; the student conserves words and keeps focus by using every sentence to indicate the sophisticated argument which will be made. The quotation from Kaplan is incorporated effectively into the sentence – thus demonstrating an understanding – and although the last sentence is very long, it is well punctuated and serves very well as a thesis statement. This introduction not only says *what* will be argued, it begins to indicate *how* it will be argued.

Student example 3

This introduction is not great. However, it does demonstrate an understanding of the essay question, presenting what philosophy lecturers often refer to as an exposition (or outline) of the main philosophical idea – moral relativism – under interrogation. The context provided is useful in that it becomes integral in understanding two premises moral relativism is based on; the strategies used to introduce these – 'firstly... secondly...' – shows the writer is in control of the material. Having said this, this introduction does not indicate any kind of ultimate argument that the essay will be following. It merely concentrates on introducing moral relativism as a theory – so it does not introduce the argument the essay will follow. This could have been easily done by interrogating the quotation in the question, and eventually producing a sentence beginning as such: 'Whilst it could be understood that moral relativism is incoherent <FOR THESE REASONS> it will also be shown that <ARGUMENT>.' In other words, the thesis statement in an introduction does not necessarily have to be a straightforward agreement or disagreement with the statement in the question. It could be a complication, but it has to indicate that a conclusion has been reached, and so tell the reader what the essay will be aiming to show.

Exercise on page 104

Student example 1

This works quite well as a focused conclusion to a short essay. The student demonstrates a good understanding of the Terry Eagleton quotation – a passage which begins the conclusion effectively as it almost sums up the argument the student makes, and so puts this argument within a wider critical debate. It shows an independence of mind, moreover, that the student also critiques Eagleton's extreme characterisation of the situation. The conclusion seems to reiterate the main argument about the play, and perhaps goes on to think of the wider implications of this, in the last sentence, by presenting a theory about the danger of telling one's own story in any context. However, the wider implications could have been explored more directly, and in more depth, making the conclusion ultimately more sophisticated and wide-ranging.

Student example 2

This conclusion certainly fulfils the role of concluding the argument and answering the original question. It presents a really clear summary of the pros and cons of the anthropological method: Mass Oberservation. What is more impressive, is the way it questions the implications of the question, saying that although there were flaws with this anthropological method, it would be unfair to focus upon them too heavily, because the method needs to be put into a historical context, and considerations about the materials available at the time need to be made. The conclusion does read as though it is a mini version of the essay, however, which does not make it that interesting to read. As mentioned, it is difficult to write a conclusion which is not simply repeating points from the essay; the part where the more 'ideal' method was outlined was leading towards a more interesting conclusion. Perhaps, a more assertive start to the conclusion would make clear the final argument, something like:

> To conclude, although there are many flaws with Mass Observation as an anthropological method, it would be unfair to dismiss it out of hand. Firstly, it did provide some valuable data, unobtainable elsewhere... Secondly, more rigorous methods would rely on technology not available at the time, and might be considered more intrusive...

Student example 3

This is a very good conclusion. It sums up the essay topic, emphasising the main critique of Blair's approach – he is evoking universal values, without allowing for them to be formed by all who are going to adopt them (or be expected to live by them). The logic of this argument is reiterated, and then the argument against Blair is articulated in direct, effective terms. The writer not only critiques Blair but suggests what he thinks he *should* be doing, to remain consistent with his chosen value system. To have a recommendation like this in a conclusion shows an independent critical mind, and successfully enables the conclusion to widen the debate, rather than close it down with a simple reiteration of the essay's argument.

● Chapter 6

Exercise on page 155

Example 1

a. This is a challenging question. It is asking you to think about how the ways representations of the relationships between the sexes can be used to explore social and political change. You will need to explain how social and political change are explored and imagined in the novels, and how analysing the different representations of the relationships between the sexes helps your understanding of this change.

b. First of all, think of the key terms in the question – the titles of the texts need to be focused on as well as the key terms for consideration, which will help structure the answer. You will need to consider what the 'feminist terms' are – this is the angle the question is taking. So, rather than thinking of the representation of gender generally, you would need to explore how 'feminists' or a feminist critical perspective would consider it. Therefore you would need to state which 'feminists' you are going to discuss. In your discussion of the representation of gender in 'feminist terms' you need to think about the difference between the representation in the two novels, thinking about whether *Wide Sargasso Sea* is an 'advance' for feminists or a 'retreat'. Because you are discussing this quotation, you will not necessarily present a question which agrees with the statement. Rather, you should consider the extent to which the representation of gender in *Wide Sargasso Sea* could be considered by some feminists to be a retreat from that presented in *Jane Eyre*. Then you would discuss the extent to which others, and *you* as the primary critical voice of the essay, agree with this opinion.

c.   This question asks you to think about gender in relation to language. You are asked to read the Virginia Woolf quotation as saying something about the relationship between language and gender. The idea of a 'man's sentence' needs to be discussed and preferably defined within the context of Woolf's theories on women's writing. In other words you need to show you understand what the quotation means before you can start using it to discuss language and gender in the two novels. Your analysis of the two novels could perhaps identify moments in which the 'man's sentence' is avoided by the women writers, or moments when the women in the novel stumble over language which is designed to empower men. But your discussion should also use an analysis of the novels to critique the Woolf quotation, evaluating its relevance to the novels and identifying points which suggest a different relationship between language and gender. Because the question focuses upon two novels, the essay may involve a discussion about how Woolf's sentiment is more suited to one than the other.

NOTE: These three questions all ask you to consider two texts. Usually the best way to answer such questions is to adopt a comparative thematic structure. This means that you would discuss a key theme in each paragraph, and all paragraphs would address both texts. Occasionally, however, it may make sense to discuss one text in isolation, before moving on to discuss the second text in relation to the first. For example, in Question b, you might choose to discuss feminism in *Jane Eyre* first in order to establish a paradigm against which *Wide Sargasso Sea* might be judged.

Example 2

1. For this question you need to imagine you are an African Christian and so consider in depth how that would mean you would think. You need to outline the argument for Christianity as a foreign religion, alien to Africans, defining the terms 'foreign' and 'alien' within a consideration of the history of Christianity in Africa. Then you would need to address the points you have made in this argument, and present your position as an African Christian, making clear what being an African Christian means, and how your Christianity fits with your status as an African citizen.

2. The word 'still' is a key word in this essay title, indicating that you will need to consider when and why Christianity was a 'foreign' religion in Africa (if indeed you think it ever was). Within your answer you need to give a history of Christianity in Africa, explore and give a working definition of the term 'foreign' and outline the main characteristics of Christianity in Africa today.

3. This question asks you to discuss the main characteristics of Christianity in contemporary Africa, but since you will be writing a critical essay you should not simply write in list form what you think they are. Your essay needs to present a discussion about what the most important characteristics of Christianity in contemporary Africa are; you need to make an argument for choosing to discuss the characteristics you do as the most important, whilst considering how Christianity in Africa may have changed (since the question is asking you to discuss the 'main' characteristics). You will need to contextualise your answer by thinking about why these are the main characteristics, what is specific about Christianity in Africa and why.

Index

Sections which incorporate exercises, examples, figures and tables are shown in **bold** type.